Adolescents and
the Media

Developmental Clinical Psychology and Psychiatry Series

Series Editor: Alan E. Kazdin, Yale University

Recent volumes in this series . . .

Adolescents and the Media

Medical and Psychological Impact

Victor C. Strasburger

Volume 33
Developmental Clinical Psychology and Psychiatry

SAGE Publications
International Educational and Professional Publisher
Thousand Oaks   London   New Delhi

Camel, Lark, Marlboro, Newports, Sega, Super Nintendo, Spuds McKenzie, and Virginia Slims are registered trademarks.

For information address:

SAGE Publications, Inc.
2455 Teller Road
Thousand Oaks, California 91320

SAGE Publications Ltd.
6 Bonhill Street
London EC2A 4PU
United Kingdom

SAGE Publications India Pvt. Ltd.
M-32 Market
Greater Kailash I
New Delhi 110 048 India

Printed in the United States of America

Library of Congress Cataloging-in-Publication Data

Strasburger, Victor C., 1949-
  Adolescents and the media: medical and psychological impact /
Victor C. Strasburger.
      p. cm. — (Developmental clinical psychology and psychiatry:
  v. 33)
  Includes bibliographical references and index.
  ISBN 0-8039-5499-9 (alk. paper). — ISBN 0-8039-5500-6 (pbk. :
alk. paper)
  1. Mass media and teenagers. I. Title. II. Series.
HQ799.2.M35S87   1995
302.23'0935—dc20   94-45245

This book is printed on acid-free paper.

95 96 97 98 99   10 9 8 7 6 5 4 3 2 1

Sage Production Editor: Diane S. Foster

For Alya, Max, and Katya, with love,
and for Dr. Michael B. Rothenberg, mentor
and friend, who figured this out long ago . . .

CONTENTS

SERIES EDITOR'S
INTRODUCTION

Interest in child development and adjustment is by no means new. Yet only recently has the study of children benefited from advances in both clinical and scientific research. Advances in the social and biological sciences, the emergence of disciplines and subdisciplines that focus exclusively on childhood and adolescence, and greater appreciation of the impact of such influences as the family, peers, and school have helped accelerate research on developmental psychopathology. Apart from interest in the study of child development and adjustment for its own sake, the need to address clinical problems of adulthood naturally draws one to investigate precursors in childhood and adolescence.

Within a relatively brief period, the study of psychopathology among children and adolescents has proliferated considerably. Several different professional journals, annual book series, and handbooks devoted entirely to the study of children and adolescents and their adjustment document the proliferation of work in the field. Nevertheless, there is a paucity of resource material that presents information in an authoritative, systematic, and disseminable fashion. There is a need within the field to convey the latest developments and to represent different disciplines, approaches, and conceptual views to the topics of childhood and adolescent adjustment and maladjustment.

The Sage Series on **Developmental Clinical Psychology and Psychiatry** is designed to serve uniquely several needs of the field. The Series encompasses individual monographs prepared by experts in the fields of clinical child psychology, child psychiatry, child development, and related disciplines. The primary focus is on developmental psychopathology, which refers broadly here to the diagnosis, assessment, treatment, and prevention of problems that arise in the period from infancy through adolescence. A working assumption of the Series is that understanding, identifying, and treating problems of youth must draw on multiple disciplines and diverse views within a given discipline.

The task for individual contributors is to present the latest theory and research on various topics that affect the adjustment and functioning of youth. Authors are asked to bridge potential theory, research, and clinical practice and to outline the current status and future directions. The goals of the Series and the tasks presented to individual contributors are demanding. We have been extremely fortunate in recruiting leaders in the fields who have been able to translate their recognized scholarship and expertise into highly readable works on contemporary topics.

The present book discusses the impact of the media on adolescents. In an authoritative, scholarly, and poignant fashion, Dr. Victor Strasburger conveys the many ways in which the media influence adolescents, multiple perspectives and conceptual views regarding how the influences occur, and the short- and long-term effects of exposure. Topics critical to mental and physical health are covered, including teenage violence, substance use (e.g., alcohol, cigarettes), suicide, sexual activity, and eating disorders and how these are and can be influenced by movies, television, and video games in their various forms. Extensive research is drawn on to convey that the impact is too significant to neglect. From this book, it is clear that the media play a role in diverse facets of at-risk behavior and adjustment. This is not to oversimplify that the media are the source of the problems but rather to draw on present evidence to ensure that deleterious influences are clearly recognized as a step toward more informed programming. To that end, several solutions are proposed to improve the impact of the media on youth.

—*Alan E. Kazdin, Ph.D.*

PREFACE

The best way to become acquainted with a subject is to write a book about it.

Benjamin Disraeli

This slim volume is not intended to be a comprehensive review of the media literature. Indeed, such a review would be a monumental task, far exceeding my abilities. Rather this book is intended to be a concise review of media effects on adolescent behavior and psychology that primary care physicians and nurses, educators, and even parents might find appealing. The communications literature is voluminous and, to the uninitiated, can be quite daunting. I hope that this volume will "demystify" it and will make a strong case for the importance of understanding the impact of the media on young people's lives.

I would like to acknowledge and thank those colleagues and friends (unnamed, but not unappreciated) who have encouraged me in this work and who understand that to be a pediatrician in the 1990s means that sensitivity to these issues is important.

1

OVERVIEW: HOW IS THE RESEARCH DONE? WHAT ARE THE ISSUES?

I believe television is going to be the test of the modern world, and that in this new opportunity to see beyond the range of our vision we shall discover either a new and unbearable disturbance of the general peace, or a soaring radiance in the sky.

Novelist E. B. White, 1938

Until television has valuable interesting programs for children, parents can simply get rid of the set. This would prevent their children from being brutalized by violence and made passive by long hours of immobilized viewing.

Pediatrician Benjamin Spock
[personal communication, 1987]

In the early part of the 20th century, parents and educators were not worried about television because electricity had not even been discovered then. But there was a different form of media that adults found equally appalling—comic books! Comic books would be the ruin of the next generation. Comic books represented a death knell to reading, an open invitation to riot and mayhem, and quite possibly the imminent decline of Western civilization. Somehow, Western civilization survived anyway.

From a historical perspective, the media have always represented a potential "threat" to society. Anything new that captures the imagination of children and adolescents and distracts them from obeying their elders certainly qualifies. Throughout the 20th century, one medium has simply replaced another as being the largest threat—first comic books, then radio, and now television, movies, rock music, music videos, and video games.

Next may be virtual reality games, 500-channel television programming, or handheld personal entertainment systems that might incorporate all of the current "threats."

But are such threats real or imagined? Are the media potentially harmful to adolescents, or do they simply provide amusement and entertainment during a period of immense development, growth, and stress? Are those who criticize the media simply "old fogies" who dislike seeing the Establishment ridiculed, or are they serious scholars who look at the social science research and see cause for alarm? And what about the New York television networks and the Hollywood entertainment industry? Are they simply pandering to popular tastes—satisfying the demand for sexier and more violent movies and TV shows—or do they *create* the demand and ignore the consequences that their products are having? This book will attempt to answer these difficult questions and others as well: Are teenagers more susceptible to the media than adults? How do they use different media? Can teenagers be taught to be media-resistant? Can prosocial media teach teenagers healthy lifestyles and decision making?

Such questions require considerable reflection. They also demand a working knowledge of communications research, normal adolescent psychology (e.g., how adolescents use the media; why they are susceptible to its influence), and at least some familiarity with current threats to the health of American youth.

COMMUNICATIONS RESEARCH

The average American child watches approximately 23 hours of TV per week; the average teenager watches nearly 22 hours per week (Nielsen Media Research, 1993). These data include network and cable viewing but do *not* include movies viewed on a videocassette recorder (VCR) or use of video and computer games. When VCR and viedo game use are added, teenagers may spend as many as 35 to 55 hours in front of the TV set (Klein et al., 1993). Such data require a context: Young people spend more time watching television than doing any other leisure time activity except sleeping and spend more time watching TV by the time they complete high school (15,000-18,000 hours) than in the classroom (12,000 hours). In fact, by the time today's children reach age 70, they will have spent 7 to 10 *years* of their lives watching television (Strasburger, 1992). More than half of all children have their own TV set. Clearly, this is a medium to be reckoned with. But how?

TABLE 1.1   Does Television's Portrayal of Sexuality Influence Teenagers?[a]
(*N* = 1,250 adults)

	Yes	No
Does TV influence values and behavior?	81	15
Is TV a positive influence?	44	40
Does TV encourage teenagers to become sexually active?	64	30[b]
Does TV give teenagers a realistic view of sex?	33	66

SOURCE: Adapted from Harris and Associates (1987).
[a] Values are represented in percentages.
[b] 3% said it discouraged them; 27% said it had no effect.

Detecting what effects, if any, television has on adolescents is a methodological "mission impossible." In medical research, for example, an unaffected group is compared with an affected group and appropriate conclusions are drawn. But where does one find an unaffected control group in media research? What children or adolescents growing up in the past several decades have not been exposed to significant amounts of television and other media? Ninety-eight percent of American households contain at least one television set, and two thirds contain two or more (Nielsen Media Research, 1993). Indeed, more households have TV sets than have indoor plumbing. Cable TV extends into 60% of American homes, and 77% of households contain a VCR (Nielsen Media Research, 1993). The ubiquitous nature of television makes it as difficult to study as the air we breathe. We can sample the air and compare it with other air samples. We can try to detect what contaminates it. We can even try to study groups of people breathing different types of air (e.g., polluted air vs. mountain air). But can we definitively conclude that one city's air causes one particular person's lung cancer?

A variety of methods have evolved to deal with this dilemma. The simplest and easiest research method has become increasingly familiar to the American public—*attitudinal surveys,* better known as opinion polls. For example, does television's portrayal of sexuality influence teenagers' actual behavior? A representative national sample of 1,250 adults, polled by Louis Harris and Associates (1987), says yes (see Table 1.1).

Although the poll itself was scientifically sound in terms of sampling techniques, the results say nothing about whether, in fact, television *does* influence teenagers' sexual behavior—only that the majority of adults surveyed *think* that it does. Unfortunately, because television is so well threaded into our everyday lives, people may not appreciate its effects, or

TABLE 1.2 Sources of Information About Birth Control for Adolescents

Source	% Teenagers (N = 1,000)
Parents	53
Television or movies[a]	25
Books or magazines[a]	23
Friends	45
Doctor or nurse	19

SOURCE: Adapted from Harris and Associates (1986).
[a] Note that 48% comes from these two categories.

alternatively, they may overreact and have inaccurate perceptions of its influence. Even so, a variety of studies indicate that the media constitute a major self-reported source of information for adolescents about both sex and drugs (Strasburger, 1990) (see Table 1.2).

Content analyses represent the next level of sophistication in media research. They, at least, can give an extremely accurate picture of what is actually being shown on television—how much sex and violence, how many alcohol advertisements, how many minority characters, and so forth. Such reports involve simply counting the depictions of a particular behavior (e.g., a main character shooting a gun or smoking). But content analyses cannot provide any index of a viewer's reaction to those depictions or any evidence regarding the effects of such depictions on actual behavior. However, exposure represents vital information. Longitudinal analyses, such as Gerbner's violence profiles at the Annenberg School for Communication (Gerbner, Morgan, & Signorielli, 1994), have been very helpful in understanding both the content of network television over a 25-year period and the dynamics of the industry's response to calls for change.

A third method of TV research has now become extinct: the _naturalistic experiment._ This technique came closest to the medical model of research and involved comparing children in communities that had television with children in communities that did not. In the Western world, the latter can no longer be found. Two naturalistic experiments, one in Australia (Murray & Kippax, 1978) and the other in British Columbia (Williams, 1986), examined communities before and after television was introduced and compared them with nearby communities with one or multiple channels available. These studies yielded very "pure" data about violence and aggressive behavior, creativity, and displacement of sports activities by television (as will be discussed in subsequent chapters).

In the early 1960s, a number of fascinating *laboratory experiments* actually constituted the earliest work on television's effects. In the laboratory, conditions could be easily manipulated and controlled. For example, one group of children could be shown a violent action program, another group a prosocial program, and a third nothing. The children's behavior at playtime could then be assessed. During the early 1960s, social science researchers were most comfortable with experimental psychology and accustomed to studying laboratory animals. These studies were often strongly conclusive but have subsequently been criticized for the artificiality of the conditions, the brevity of the TV exposure, and the short follow-up period for the effects being examined (Comstock & Strasburger, 1990). Nevertheless, they represent an important contribution to the database.

One solution to the artificiality of laboratory experiments seems to be *field experiments*, in which subjects can be studied in "real life." However, real life confounds media research because it is difficult to find comparable groups, manipulate different variables, and achieve randomization. The gain in naturalism is probably offset by a loss in confidence that whatever differences in behavior that are uncovered can be attributed to the variable being manipulated (Comstock & Strasburger, 1990). Because such studies appear to be the most true to life and are usually inconclusive, many people (especially network executives) continue to extol their virtues (see Gadow & Sprafkin, 1989; Singer, 1989; Strasburger, 1989b).

Television research progressed dramatically in the 1970s when a number of researchers undertook *correlational studies.* Given the impossibility of doing naturalistic research as television spread throughout the Western hemisphere, investigators opted to try to determine if differences existed between heavily exposed and lightly exposed groups of children and teenagers. For example, if television violence is harmful, we would expect that children who watch more of it are more profoundly influenced than children who view very little of it. Similarly, if content analyses show that violence on TV is pervasive, we would expect it to influence heavy viewers more than light viewers. But which comes first—does television violence cause aggressive behavior, or do aggressive children simply choose to watch more violent programming? This is the "chicken-and-egg" dilemma of correlational studies. The fact that two behaviors are correlated does not indicate that one causes the other. Fortunately, sophisticated statistical techniques (e.g., *partial correlations*), the use of *meta-analyses* in which the individual studies become data points in one single study,

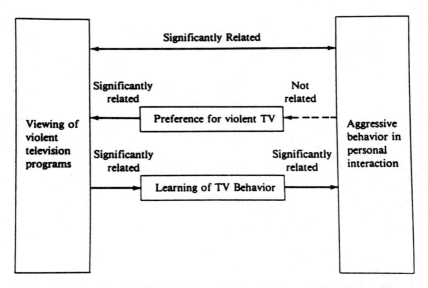

Figure 1.1. Directionality: The "Chicken-and-Egg Dilemma." Which comes first—aggressive behavior, which results in the choice of violent programs, or violent programs, which cause aggressive behavior? Longitudinal correlational studies indicate that a strong association exists between violent programming and aggressive behavior, not that aggressive children merely choose more violent programming.

SOURCE: Liebert and Sprafkin, *The early window—Effects of television on children and youth* (3rd ed.). Copyright © 1988 by Allyn and Bacon. Reprinted by permission.

and the use of *longitudinal correlational studies* have evolved to help establish more of a basis for causality (see Figure 1.1). In subsequent chapters, we will examine all of these various studies for clues about the influence of television on adolescents.

FOUR IMPORTANT PRINCIPLES

Television research has been abundant, dynamic, and varied. It would be a mistake to write off laboratory experiments because they are artificial or to dismiss field experiments because they are too imperfect. Each genre contributes unique information, and the overall pattern is what matters most. But when examining the communications literature, it is vital to remember four important principles:

1. Social science research is *not* medical research. Correlational coefficients of 0.85 in medicine are highly significant; in social science research, an *r* value of 0.40 may be highly significant.

2. There is a statistical axiom that the unreliability of measurement reduces the degree of association that can be determined. In TV research, the measures of exposure and behavior are far from being perfectly reliable.

3. Given the ubiquity of television, even "low-exposure" groups conceivably still have considerable knowledge about the exposure to TV programming. Thus whatever significant associations are found reflect a very narrow range of TV exposure and could be considerably greater if truly low-exposure subjects could be found.

4. Primary care practitioners should not be dismayed by the complexity of TV research methodology or the seeming inability of the scientific community to agree on what it all means. Even if the vast body of TV research was inconclusive—which it is not—is a scientific study necessary to demonstrate that 5-year-olds should not be witnessing graphic violence on television? There are a variety of other grounds besides scientific ones for objecting to the various programming practices—moral, common sense, philosophical, and aesthetic. As former Federal Communications Commission (FCC) Chairman Nicholas Johnson once remarked, "All television is educational television. The only question is, 'What is it teaching?'" (Strasburger, 1985, p. 18).

HOW ADOLESCENTS
LEARN FROM TELEVISION

Television is a powerful medium, and young people are uniquely susceptible to it. Many studies have demonstrated television's ability to transmit information and to shape social attitudes. Television can:

- Influence viewers' perceptions of what constitutes the "real world" and normal social behavior (Bandura, 1977; Hawkins & Pingree, 1982)
- Help to mold cultural norms (Gerbner, 1985; Greenberg, 1982)
- Convey important and believable messages about the behaviors it depicts (Bandura, 1977; Roberts, 1982)

Adolescents' attitudes are malleable and TV can give teenagers their first real glimpse into the secretive adult world of sex, drugs, and success long before they are able to learn about it firsthand (Myerowitz, 1982). Television gives teenagers "scripts" about how adults are supposed to act; it teaches them about gender roles, conflict resolution, patterns of courtship and sexual gratification, and methods of coping with stress (Gagnon & Simon, 1987; Silverman-Watkins, 1983).

But how does television actually affect children and adolescents' *behavior?* This is an area of some controversy that involves theories, not facts, although many of the theories are extremely persuasive and have data to support them. In addition, many of the theories are interrelated and mutually compatible. Chief among them has been the *social learning theory* (Bandura, 1973, 1978, 1994). In 1963, Stanford University psychologist Albert Bandura diverged from the prevailing psychoanalytical notion that children's personalities develop as a result of sexual conflicts and theorized that children learn behavior by observing others directly in real life and vicariously through the media. Certainly, television is rife with attractive adult role models for children and teenagers. Indeed, the most effective way for parents to teach children certain behaviors is to demonstrate the behavior and have the children model themselves after it—precisely what television does. What is observed may be imitated, or it may simply influence a child's beliefs about the world. Modeling may be a crucial factor in teenagers' decisions about when and how to begin consuming alcohol, for example. Sports and rock stars frequently appear in beer and wine ads, and the underlying messages are clear: "Real men" drink beer; beer drinkers have more fun, more friends, and are sexier; and consuming alcohol is the norm rather than the exception (Strasburger, 1993b).

Three other theories most applicable to children and adolescents are Zillmann's *excitation* or *arousal theory* (1971), Berkowitz's *cognitive neoassociation theory* (1984), and Huesmann's *theory of cognitive scripting* (1986). The first, which is more relevant to younger children, holds that excitement produced by media exposure may transfer to other ongoing activities, thus heightening the intensity of whatever emotion is in play at the time. The second holds that vicarious media experiences may either encourage or inhibit behavior by evoking certain associations, images, or thoughts. And the third theory proposes that television programs provide young people with behavioral scripts that can be retrieved at any time. Retrieval depends on the similarity between the real situation at hand and the fictional event, as well as the circumstances surrounding when the script was first encoded.

Imitation of media-displayed behaviors may be direct and immediate, or it may be delayed and more subtle. When imitation is direct and immediate, it often makes headlines. In 1961, Schramm, Lyle, and Parker (1961) documented numerous cases in which television was implicated in antisocial behavior committed by youths. In 1976, pediatric medical literature described three case reports of children severely injured while imitating the stunts of motorcycle daredevil Evel Knievel (Daven, O'Conner, & Briggs, 1976). When two well-known television medical reporters responded to a landmark article in the prestigious *New England Journal of Medicine* about television violence (Somers, 1976) by calling for letters from readers of the journal, they were deluged with more than 1,500 responses, most from pediatricians and psychiatrists with anecdotal information concerning imitative injuries (Feingold & Johnson, 1977). More recently, several teenagers were killed after imitating a scene from *Stand By Me,* a movie in which the main characters successfully dodge an oncoming train by jumping off a bridge. And three teenagers were killed and two injured after imitating a similar scene in *The Program,* a Disney film in which a depressed and drunken football player lies down in the middle of a highway (James, 1993). The studio excised the latter scene from the movie, which was already in circulation.

Not only are direct learning and copying from models important, but so is *generalization.* In other words, a violent program might lead to the display of other responses of a similar nature. Understanding *instigation and cue theory* (Berkowitz's cognitive neoassociation theory)—what facilitates or inhibits certain behaviors—is actually a key component of social learning theory as well. Berkowitz (1962, 1964, 1973) theorized that whether depicted violence is *justified,* for example, becomes a key determinant in whether it will be adapted. Observing justified violence is more likely to "cue" aggressive modeling in the viewer. Unfortunately, there is no more prevalent notion on American television today than that of justified violence (Comstock & Strasburger, 1993). This corollary of social learning theory is more sensitive to the notion that children and adolescents may therefore learn aggressive attitudes from certain programs because violence is usually portrayed as a necessary and acceptable solution as long as the "good guy" triumphs.

One theory about TV's effects that has essentially been discredited is the *catharsis theory.* In his *Poetics,* Aristotle suggested that spectators could be purged of their feelings of grief, fear, or pity vicariously. The idea that aggressive impulses could be purged through exposure to fantasy violence emanated from psychoanalytic theories claiming that various "energies" coursed through the body like ancient "humours," requiring release. Network executives have long hoped that this theory would hold true because all of the violence and sex on American television could then be considered therapeutic. Unfortunately, to date, the preponderance of data suggests that no catharsis occurs among television viewers (Berkowitz &

Rawlings, 1963; Comstock & Strasburger, 1990; Ellis & Sekrya, 1972; Gunter, 1994; Huesmann, 1982, 1986).

What is even more important to understand than which theory or theories are "correct" about how television influences young viewers is the manner in which TV works. The vast majority of television's influence is indirect, subtle, and cumulative—*not* immediate and direct. One group of researchers refers to this as "stalagmite effects—cognitive deposits built up almost imperceptibly from the drip-drip-drip of television's electronic limewater" (Bryant & Rockwell, 1994, p. 183). Greenberg (1988) suggested that occasionally the drip model should be replaced by a "drench" model—a particularly popular program such as *The Cosby Show* can completely overwhelm all previous portrayals of blacks on television, for example.

Many studies have demonstrated support for the *cultivation hypothesis* (Gerbner, Gross, Morgan, & Signorielli, 1994)—people who view large amounts of television are more likely to believe that TV depicts the real world, or that the real world should conform to television's rules. In other words, television and other media change the way people view their own world. For example, Gerbner, Gross, Morgan, and Signorielli's studies (1980b, 1986) of the "Mean World Syndrome" demonstrate that heavy viewers consistently view the world the way it is portrayed on TV, thus dramatically overestimating their risk of being involved in a violent crime or knowing the actual number of criminals in society. As anchorman Howard Beale yells to his television audience in Paddy Cheyevsky's *Network*:

> You people sit there, night after night. You're beginning to think the tube is reality and your own lives are unreal. This is mass madness!

Singer, Singer, and Rapaczynski (1984) demonstrated a similar "mean and scary world syndrome" in children who watch large amounts of television. Other experiments have shown that even brief exposure to violent programming can make a child more tolerant of other children's aggression (Drabman & Thomas, 1974), and that a heavy diet of viewing violence can be associated with attitudes favoring the use of violence (Greenberg, 1975).

Mainstreaming represents a similar type of force at work: Because television contains a fairly uniform set of social messages, television viewers' social *schema* tend to be whittled down to a small set of similar beliefs. For example, because the numbers of doctors, lawyers, and policemen are overrepresented on American television, adolescent males may develop the mistaken impression that only professionals have value in adult society, not blue-collar workers. Likewise, adolescent females may be selling themselves short on the basis of what they see on TV. This could help to explain Gilligan's (1990) findings that young adolescent girls seem to lose some of the self-esteem they have developed throughout childhood. A 1988 report (Steenland, 1988) that examined more than 200 episodes of programs containing adolescent characters found:

- Teenage girls' looks are portrayed as being more important than their brains.
- Intelligent girls are sometimes depicted as being social misfits.
- Teenage girls are more passive than their male counterparts on TV.
- TV frequently portrays teenage girls as being obsessed with shopping, grooming, and dating and incapable of having serious conversations about academic interests or career goals.
- Ninety-four percent of teenage girls on TV are middle class or wealthy.

American teenagers of both sexes may, in fact, suffer from a "Sexy World Syndrome" (Strasburger, 1989a). One survey of teenagers found that they felt TV was equally or more encouraging about sex than their best male or female friends (Brown, Childers, & Waszak, 1989). When college students were asked to identify models of responsible and irresponsible sexual behavior, they selected primarily media figures; those who selected them as models of sexual *responsibility* had higher rates of sexual activity themselves and more permissive attitudes (Fabes & Strouse, 1984, 1987). In another study, pregnant teenagers were twice as likely to think that TV relationships are "real" than nonpregnant teens and that TV characters would not use contraception if involved in a sexual relationship (Corder-Bolz, 1981).

Do researchers consider children and adolescents the same when studying the impact of the media? Certainly not. Although much of the vast television research literature comes from studies done with children, many significant studies have involved adolescents. Clearly, children process television differently: They are less able to understand the fine points of plot, characterization, and motivation (Bryant & Anderson, 1983). Very young children cannot even distinguish between commercials and regular programs (Atkin, 1982; Liebert & Sprafkin, 1988). However, notions learned by children could conceivably result in behavioral consequences when they are adolescents (Strasburger, 1993a). With violence and aggressive behavior, this is almost certainly the case (Eron, 1995; Huesmann, 1982). The years between ages 2 and 8 are crucial in determining attitudes about violence. With sexual behavior or alcohol advertising, the window of vulnerability may be somewhat later—the preteenage and early adolescent years, for example. In some respects, *young teenagers* may be the most susceptible population to television's hidden themes and messages because their identities and attitudes are evolving and more malleable.

SIX IMPORTANT PROPOSITIONS

Underlying the chapters that follow are six important propositions that will be important to recognize before beginning the discussion of the data.

1. Teenagers are neither big children nor small adults. They have their own unique physiology and psychology. As such, they may be uniquely susceptible to the influence of television and other media.

Adults sometimes forget that in a very short time span adolescents must accomplish a bewildering number of major tasks (Strasburger & Brown, 1991):

- Establish a sense of identity
- Establish independence from parents
- Learn to establish relationships with one's peers and with the opposite sex
- Finish formal schooling
- Begin to assess one's place in modern society and formulate plans for a career or job

Accomplishing these tasks involves obtaining input and guidance from whatever opportunities arise, whether they are officially sanctioned (e.g., sex or drug education programs at school or church) or merely readily available (the peer group). Although newer research indicates that as many as 80% of teenagers survive their adolescence with minimal or no turmoil (Offer, Ostrov, & Howard, 1989), these years are still confusing ones for many young people. Virtually all of the previous tasks add up to one major question: "How (and when) do I become an adult?" With its abundance of attractive adult role models, television provides a vast library of information regarding the adult world and how adults behave. Until children are old enough to understand that television is fantasy—and, sadly, many adults cannot even accomplish this task—young people are likely to be heavily influenced by the programming they view. This may be especially true if important adult role models are absent from the home (single parent families, children of divorce, etc.). In a sense, television functions as a "super peer group" with all the potential for influencing behavior that this entails. It is also an important source of information for teenagers about sex and drugs and may be the leading source if they do not receive such instruction at home, school, or church.

One new development in communications research is an understanding that different viewers may process the same content differently. Although adolescence is widely perceived to be a time of rapid change, most teens probably deal with one issue at a time (Coleman, 1978). Therefore, their vulnerability to different media themes could depend on which issue occupies center stage at any particular time. In addition, teenagers' own developmental differences probably play a role, as do interpretational differences based on age, race, sex, or experience (Brown et al., 1989; Christenson & Roberts, 1990). One traditional concern is that the media present a great deal of information in a "disinterested" fashion and that when young people seek entertainment, they are less well-defended against—and therefore more susceptible to—content that may not match their own beliefs and values (Christenson & Roberts, 1990).

2. Even if the health consequences of too much sex, violence, and alcohol on television could not be demonstrated in neatly controlled scientific studies, virtually no arguments (other than some oblique First Amendment concerns) are *in favor* of exposing young people to such programming.

The quality and quantity of the scientific studies vary regarding the effect of television on various aspects of adolescent behavior. The connection between media violence and aggressive behavior has been established beyond a reasonable doubt (Comstock & Strasburger, 1993; Geen, 1994; Huston et al., 1992), but only a paucity of data exists regarding sexual activity, for example. Given the number and the nature of the studies about media violence, the influence of television can probably be extrapolated to other areas of adolescent behavior. However, social science research is far from perfect, and asking for the type of "scientific proof" analogous to Group A streptococcal bacteria causing acute rheumatic fever may be foolhardy and may represent a misreading of what social science research can and cannot accomplish. Most pediatricians, child psychologists and psychiatrists, public health specialists, and parents would acknowledge that too much graphic violence and sex on television cannot be very useful to young people. At some point, pure science must give way to common sense and to a societal sense of maternalism, paternalism, and public health.

Although many people raise First Amendment concerns when this issue is discussed, there are a number of considerations: (1) television *is* regulated under the Communications Act of 1934 and the FCC, (2) free speech is *not* entirely unabridged (e.g., yelling fire in a crowded theater, inciting to riot, etc.), and (3) advertising is considered in a separate category from free speech because it is business related, and advertising that is false, deceptive, or contrary to the public health is *not* protected by the First Amendment (Shiffrin, 1993).

3. Hollywood and the networks are doing more than simply entertaining the American public and giving it what it wants. The media teach young people important messages that sometimes have very real and adverse health consequences.

There are many reasons for the controversy surrounding television research, ranging from a simple misunderstanding of the literature to capitalistic greed. (Even in 1993, when the networks were continuing to lose some of their audience share to cable, they still grossed $11 billion [Johnson, 1993].) But one of the primary reasons for the controversy is that adults do not understand and refuse to believe that children view television differently than themselves. Most adults recognize that television is fantasy, entertainment, often unreal. Children are not capable of such discrimination. Therefore, the industry argument that "no one takes this stuff seriously" (see National Council for Families & Television, 1994) may be at least arguable for adults but is completely erroneous when considering young people. Indeed, the industry often cites important work such as *Schindler's List* as being prohumanitarian, or *The Cosby Show* for showing strong family values, but then denies that any programming can have negative effects (Medved, 1992). On the other hand, expecting the industry to acknowledge the connection between media violence and real-life violence may be about as reasonable as expecting tobacco company executives to admit that cigarette smoking causes cancer (Centerwall, 1992a, 1992b).

Similarly, Hollywood's traditional argument that it merely serves as supplier to the public's demand for violence does not hold up either. As Gerbner et al. (1994) note:

Television violence is an overkill of 'happy violence'—swift, cool, effective, without tragic consequences and in other ways divorced from real life and crime statistics. "Happy violence" is the byproduct of a manufacturing and marketing process that defies popular taste and imposes uniformity on creative people and viewers. (Gerbner, Morgan, & Signorielli, 1994)

There is no evidence that viewers want violent programming. In fact, there is significant evidence to the contrary. Gerbner et al. (1994) compared Nielsen ratings of two samples containing more than 100 programs each—one of violent programs, the other of programs without violence. The nonviolent programs had a higher overall rating and market share. Similarly, a movie industry study found that PG-rated movies were three times more likely to gross $100 million than R-rated films (Giles & Fleming, 1993). Public opinion polls also show that the American public is increasingly opposed to the amount of violence it views. A 1993 poll of more than 1,500 adults nationwide found that 80% believe entertainment violence is harmful to society. An earlier poll from 1989 revealed that more than 50% believe exposure to media violence makes people more likely to commit violence.

The current generation of adolescents faces health threats unparalleled in the history of the United States (see Rosen, Xiangdong, & Blum, 1990; Strasburger, 1993c). *Any* influence that contributes even a small amount to the levels of violence, sexual activity, or drug taking among children and adolescents needs to be examined carefully and taken seriously. Consider the following data from the National Adolescent Student Health Survey (Centers for Disease Control, 1989), which studied a random sample of more than 11,000 8th- and 10th-grade students in 20 states:

- Forty-four percent of students reported riding with a driver who had used alcohol or drugs before driving.
- Half of the boys and more than one fourth of the girls had been involved in at least one physical fight in the previous year.
- Twenty-five percent of the girls reported that someone had tried to force them to have sexual relations during the past year.
- Twenty-three percent of the boys reported having carried a knife at least once in the past year, and 7% reported carrying it daily. Nearly two thirds reported using a gun for any reason.
- Forty-two percent of the girls and 25% of the boys reported having seriously considered suicide at some time during their lives; 18% of the girls and 11% of the boys had attempted suicide.
- Nearly half of all the students surveyed thought that donating blood increases the likelihood of becoming infected with HIV; more than half were unsure or believed that "washing after having sex" decreases the likelihood of infection.

Television is hardly the sole source of these problems, nor is it even the leading source. But, as we shall see, television does make important contributions to these crucial areas of adolescent health and development. In addition, television is also the one influence that could be changed virtually overnight.

4. American television is more than just a mirror reflecting American society, which is an argument the industry frequently uses. The amount of violence and casual sex on American television is drastically out of proportion to real life. In addition, the penetration of American television and movies into everyday life is so great that "receiving Hollywood's message is no longer a matter of choice" (Medved, 1992, p. 269).

The average American child will view more than 200,000 acts of violence by the time he or she reaches age 18 (Huston et al., 1992). As one critic notes:

> It's not enough to say that Shakespeare and Marlowe were violent and civilization still survived. Technology has brought a new amplification effect into play. Never before has so much violence been shown so graphically to so many. (Morganstern, 1972)[1]

In addition to unprecedented levels of violence, the networks broadcast approximately 65,000 sexual references, innuendoes, and jokes per year during primetime and afternoon periods alone (Harris & Associates, 1988). Although American society has become more violent and American culture has tolerated more explicit sexuality, these numbers are drastically out of proportion. This is the first time in history that children have been born into a symbolic world that does not originate with their parents, church, or school (Gerbner, 1985, 1992). According to Gerbner, "We experience the world through stories. Whomever tells stories of a culture defines the terms and the agenda of human discourse and the common issues we face" (Gerbner, 1985, p. 822).

5. Television is neither "good" nor "bad." It is what we, as a society, make it.

Television can have powerful prosocial influences (for a good review, see Liebert & Sprafkin, 1988) or major negative health consequences, as we shall review. Given television's ability to entertain, inform, and enlighten in a prosocial fashion, it is *not* the intrinsically evil medium that some critics have labeled it (see Healy, 1990; Postman, 1985; Winn, 1987). The tragedy of American television is that it is 90% potentially harmful to children and only 10% prosocially useful when, in fact, these percentages would be reversed in a responsible society.

The one exception to television as an intrinsically neutral medium (which can potentially be "good" or "bad," depending on the quality of the programming) is the *displacement effect*. Clearly, television displaces more physical activities, for example, recreational sports, (Williams, 1986). If the average American child spends more than 23 hours a week watching television, that means 23 hours have not been spent playing with friends, reading, or doing homework.

6. Sadly, the television industry has lost touch with both its constituency and its founding principles. In the 1990s, American television programming exists primarily to deliver an audience with just the right demographic composition to a corresponding advertiser (Huston et al., 1992; Strasburger, 1993a).

Although the United States was the first nation in the world to have television, it is unique in lacking any clear public policy regarding it (Huston et al., 1992; Palmer, 1988). American television is regulated according to the Communications Act, passed by Congress in 1934. The preamble to the act states that the public owns the airwaves, which are leased to the networks to produce programming in the public's best interests. In the following chapters, we will examine how television programming affects adolescents in the crucial health-related areas of violence, sex and sexuality, drugs, and nutrition. After reading these chapters, it will be up to the reader to decide whether the industry is fulfilling its originally stated mission of serving the public interest.

NOTE

1. From NEWSWEEK, Feburary 14, 1972. © 1972 Newsweek, Inc. All rights reserved. Reprinted with permission.

2

MEDIA VIOLENCE AND AGGRESSIVE BEHAVIOR

Serious aggression never occurs unless there is a convergence of large numbers of causes, but one of the very important facts we have identified is exposure to media violence. . . . If we don't do something, we are contributing to a society that will be more and more violent.

Psychologist L. Rowell Huesmann

Maybe we need the catharsis of bloodletting and decapitation, like the ancient Romans needed it, as ritual. . . .

Director Martin Scorcese

If parents could package psychological influences to administer in regular doses to their children, I doubt that many would deliberately select Western gunslingers, hopped-up psychopaths, deranged sadists, slap-stick buffoons and the like, unless they entertained rather peculiar ambitions for their growing offspring. Yet such examples of behavior are delivered in quantity, with no direct charge, to millions of households daily. Harried parents can easily turn off demanding children by turning on a television set; as a result, today's youth is being raised on a heavy dosage of televised aggression and violence.

TV researcher Albert Bandura

INTRODUCTION

Violence in the United States threatens the very fabric of contemporary society. At least 2.2 million people are victims of violent injury each year,

AUTHOR'S NOTE: I am indebted to Dr. George Comstock for his major contributions to my knowledge and to this chapter.

and among adolescents, homicides and suicides rank as the second- and third-leading causes of death after motor vehicle accidents (U.S. Department of Health and Human Services, 1990). In Louisiana and Texas, more people die from gun-related injuries than from motor vehicle accidents (Centers for Disease Control, 1992c). The United States ranks first among industrialized nations in violent death rates, and for African Americans ages 15 to 34, homicide has become the leading cause of death (U.S. Department of Health and Human Services, 1990). Among teens, the suicide rate has tripled in the past 3 decades (Centers for Disease Control, 1987), more than 1 in 4 adult women report having been sexually assaulted at some time during their childhood or young adulthood (Hayes, 1987), and 2 to 4 million women are physically battered each year (U.S. Department of Health and Human Services, 1990). Is it a coincidence that as American media have become increasingly graphically violent, American society has as well? Or are the media merely "mirroring" changes in society?

More than 1,000 studies and reviews in the literature point to media violence as one *cause* of real-life violence (Strasburger, 1993a). Although media violence is certainly not the leading cause of real-life violence, it is a *significant factor*—and one that is far more easily modifiable than, for example, poverty, racism, sexism, individual psychological differences, or the quality of parenting. Virtually all of these separate studies and reviews conclude that media violence may (1) facilitate aggressive and antisocial behavior, (2) desensitize viewers to violence, and (3) increase viewers' perceptions that they are living in a mean and dangerous world (Comstock, 1991; Gerbner, 1992). Both the 1972 Surgeon General's report and the 1982 National Institute of Mental Health report concluded that exposure to media violence can increase aggressive behavior in young people (Pearl, 1982; Surgeon General's Scientific Advisory Committee, 1972). As one leading researcher recently reported: "The scientific debate is over" (Eron, 1993). Certainly, as we examine the relevant research, the reader will notice that the vast majority of it is 10 to 20 years old. This is because researchers in the field feel, as Eron does, that the basic connection has been proved beyond a reasonable doubt.

SIZE OF THE EFFECT

How much does media violence contribute to real-life violence? When 22 separate estimates of effect size were collated from various surveys, the size of the effect was approximately 5% to 15% (Comstock, 1986; Comstock & Strasburger, 1990). But this may represent a significant *underestimate.*

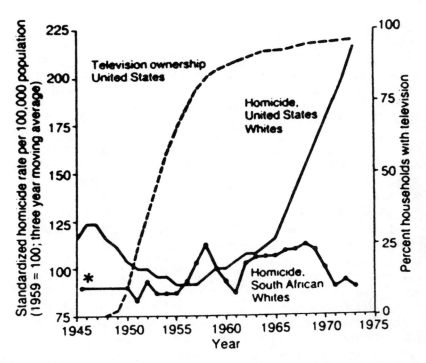

Figure 2.1. Results of a unique naturalistic study by Centerwall (1992b) comparing homicide rates in the United States and South Africa according to when TV was introduced (in the 1950s in the United States, but not until 1975 in South Africa).
SOURCE: Centerwall, 1992. © Academic Press. Reprinted with permission.

One researcher (Centerwall, 1992a, 1992b) asserts that long-term expo-sure to television is a causal factor in approximately half of all homicides in the United States; therefore, 10,000 homicides could be prevented annually if television were less violent. Centerwall examined white homi-cide and larceny rates in South Africa, Canada, and the United States and found that for the latter two countries, 10 to 15 years elapsed between the introduction of television and a subsequent doubling of the homicide and the larceny rate—exactly what one would expect if TV violence primarily affects children (see Figure 2.1). In addition, exactly as predicted, (a) urban homicide rates rose before rural rates (television was introduced into urban areas first), (b) homicide rates rose first among affluent whites (minorities could not afford early TV sets), and (c) homicide rates increased

TABLE 2.1 Violent Dramatic Programming on Network and Cable TV

| | Cable Programming | | Network Programming | |
	Children's	General	Children's	Primetime
% programs with violence	77	70	83	74
No. violent acts/hour	17	9	32	4

SOURCE: Gerbner, Morgan, & Signorielli (1994). Adapted with permissioin.

earlier in those geographical regions where TV was first introduced. South Africa was used as a "control" nation because it most resembles Western countries, yet it did not have any television until 1973. Predictably, homicide rates in South Africa have now begun to climb as well. A separate but similar study of larceny in the United States found similar results (Hennigan et al., 1982).

HOW VIOLENT IS AMERICAN TV?

American television and movies are the most violent in the world. Conservative estimates indicate that the average American child or teenager views 1,000 murders, rapes, and aggravated assaults per year on television alone (Rothenberg, 1975). A more recent review by the American Psychological Association puts this figure at 10,000 per year—or approximately 200,000 by the time a child reaches age 18 (Huston et al., 1992). If anything, children's programming is even more violent than primetime programming, and the amount of violence has not changed appreciably over the past 2 decades, despite increasing public awareness and concern (see Table 2.1). Between 1982 and 1988, the amount of television time devoted to war cartoons increased from 90 minutes to 27 hours a week (Carlsson-Paige & Levin, 1991). The recent "reality-based" shows are extremely violent (e.g., *Top Cops*). In addition, more than half of music videos on Music Television (MTV)—a medium unique in its appeal to teenagers and preteens—contain violence (Sherman & Dominick, 1986). see p. 45

note

Graphic violence is far more common in movies than on television, but the average American child watches only one or two movies per week, compared with 23 to 28 hours of TV (Nielsen Media Research, 1993). However, movies are eventually screened on broadcast TV and pay-cable channels or rented from video stores. The amount of movie violence escalates with the number of each sequel: Fatalities in *RoboCop2* increased from 32 in the original to 81; Die Hard 2 had a body count of 264, compared with 18 in *Die Hard* (Plagens et al., 1991). Film critic Roger Ebert estimates that Arnold Schwarzenegger has already "killed" 250 people on-screen during his brief movie career (Ebert, 1993). Unlike the movie ratings in every other country in the world, American movie ratings are typically based on sexual content more than the amount or explicitness of violence (Federman, 1993). In one survey of Ohio elementary school children, 20% of 5- to 7-year-olds had seen the R-rated film *Friday the 13th* (David, 1993).

THE EARLY RESEARCH

Most early research on the effects of television involved studying children in a laboratory setting. In their classic experiments, Bandura, Ross, and Ross (1963) observed the behavior of nursery school children in a playroom filled with toys, among them a Bobo doll (a punching bag with a sand base and a red nose that squeaked). The purpose of the experiment was to investigate the circumstances under which the children would learn and imitate novel aggressive acts. To explain modeling behavior fully, Bandura wanted to distinguish between the child's acquisition of new behaviors and the actual performance of them.

In one experiment, each child was first mildly frustrated by being taken away from a room full of attractive toys. While the children in the control condition were excluded, each child in the experimental group watched a filmed sequence on a simulated TV set:

> The film began with a scene in which [an adult male] model walked up to an adult-size plastic Bobo doll and ordered him to clear the way. After glaring for a moment at the noncompliant antagonist the model exhibited four novel aggressive responses, each accompanied by a distinctive verbalization. First, the model laid the Bobo doll on its side, sat on it, and punched it in the nose while remarking, "Pow, right in the nose, boom, boom." The model then raised the doll and pommeled it on the head with a mallet. Each response was accompanied by the verbalization, "Sockeroo . . . stay down." Following the mallet aggression, the model kicked the doll about the room, and these responses were interspersed with the comment, "Fly away." Finally, the model threw rubber balls at the Bobo doll, each strike punctuated with "Bang." This sequence of physically and verbally aggressive behavior was repeated twice. (Bandura, 1965, pp. 590-591)

The children in the experimental group were then subdivided according to one of three conditions: (a) a model-rewarded group who viewed the bully being rewarded with candy, (b) a model-punished group who saw the bully reprimanded, and (c) a neutral group who saw no further film. After this, each child was brought into the playroom that contained the plastic Bobo doll, three balls, a mallet, a doll house, and other toys—giving them the opportunity to display imitative, aggressive behavior (modeling); nonimitative but aggressive play (generalization or disinhibition); or nonimitative, nonaggressive play. Observers behind one-way mirrors coded the behavior, although they did not know which children had been assigned to which groups. Children in the model-rewarded and neutral groups showed a considerable number of imitative behaviors; children in the model-punished group displayed little imitation. Control children displayed few or none of the behaviors.

According to social learning theory, all of the experimental group children had learned the aggressive responses and could perform them if the circumstances were right. This was demonstrated in a subsequent experiment in which the same children were then invited to reproduce as many of the aggressive acts as they could recall and given a treat for each one. The children displayed very high rates of recall, including the model-punished group. Other Bobo doll studies showed that children could learn novel aggressive responses as easily from a cartoon-like figure, a "Cat Lady," for example, as from a human adult (Bandura et al., 1963)—a result that clearly implicates Saturday morning TV as an unhealthy reservoir of violence (Singer, 1985b).

Other researchers adapted the Bobo technology to their own experiments: One found that children exposed to aggressive sequences could reproduce them on request up to 6 to 8 months later (Hicks, 1965). Several others found that preschoolers would spontaneously aggress against a human adult dressed as a clown (Hanratty, O'Neal, & Sulzer, 1972; Hicks, 1968; Savitsky, Rogers, Izard, & Liebert, 1971). These researchers addressed the criticism that the Bobo experiments had no external validity (i.e., the attacks were simply made against an inflated toy and had no relationship to adult aggression of any kind). The validity of the Bobo doll experiments was further strengthened in a later experiment by Steuer, who had nursery school children watch ordinary violent TV programs during their breaks and found that they displayed more aggressiveness on the playground than children who had viewed nonviolent programs (Steuer, Applefield, & Smith, 1971).

Other early experiments examined whether a violent program might lead to aggressive but nonimitative behavior (i.e., generalization or disinhibition). In a 1961 experiment, nursery school children's play was assessed after they viewed either a violent cartoon or a prosocial film about a mother bear and her three babies playing together (Lovaas, 1961). Children were then given two toys to play with—one with a lever that caused one doll to hit another doll over the head with a stick, the other involving a wooden ball that maneuvered through obstacles inside a cage. Children who viewed the cartoon used the hitting doll more frequently: Disinhibition had occurred.

Because many TV programs display aggression as a means of obtaining power and rewards, experiments that examine attitudinal change and the consequences of aggression are also relevant. Bandura et al. (1963) manipulated film sequences involving two young adults identified as Rocky and Johnny. In one version, Rocky steals Johnny's toys and is rewarded; in the other, Johnny successfully defends himself and thrashes Rocky. Preschoolers who viewed the aggressor rewarded were far more aggressive themselves. When asked whom they would choose to emulate, 60% of the children who saw Rocky rewarded selected him as a model, compared to only 20% who saw him punished. Socially reprehensible behavior was being modeled as long as it was *successful*. The researchers were demonstrating that behavior is a function not only of observation but of perceived *efficacy* as well.

Berkowitz, also interested in the social learning approach, theorized that exposure to violent programming instigates an immediate aggressive response, presumably because of arousal and provocation (Berkowitz, 1962, 1964, 1973). In particular, an already aroused viewer will find justification to behave violently if he or she witnesses violence in the media. Whether the depicted aggression is *justified* also becomes a crucial determinant in whether the modeled violent behavior will be *adapted*. Justified violence is more likely to "cue" aggressive behavior. In later writings, Berkowitz amplified his theories, giving greater weight to how viewers process what they see (Berkowitz, 1984; Jo & Berkowitz, 1994). For example, their social beliefs or value systems might mitigate for or against imitation. Newer research on the impact of sexy media on adolescents supports this concept as well (Brown & Schulze, 1990; Walsh-Childers, 1991; see Chapter 3).

Experiments using younger children have come to have important implications for adolescent behavior because they have identified the circumstances under which TV can trigger aggressive or antisocial behavior. Such circumstances include:

1. Rewarding or failing to punish the aggressor
2. Portrayal of the violence as being justified

3. Aspects of the fictional portrayal that coincide with real life (e.g., the victim has traits similar to someone in real life whom the viewer dislikes)
4. Portrayal of the aggressor as being similar to the viewer
5. Depiction of violence without consequences
6. Real-life violence
7. Uncriticized violence
8. Violence without associated humor in the story
9. Aggression against females by males engaged in sexual conquest
10. Portrayals—whether violent or not—that leave the viewer in an aroused state
11. Viewers who are angry or provoked before viewing a violent portrayal (Comstock & Strasburger, 1990)

But the major contribution of experiments involving cue and instigation theory delineates exactly how American media violence may be affecting young people: As long as violence is seen as a necessary and acceptable solution to complex problems and the "good guys" triumph, it is strongly reinforced.

A UNIQUE NATURALISTIC STUDY

In 1986, Williams reported an unusual study comparing a town that had no television ("Notel") in Canada with nearby communities that received either one station ("Unitel") or multiple stations ("Multitel") (see Figure 2.2). These three communities were practically identical except for the presence of television, and data could be collected on children in Notel 2 years before and after TV was introduced. In each town, researchers obtained teachers' ratings, self-reports, and their own measures of students' physical and verbal aggressiveness. Initially lower in aggressiveness than students in Unitel or Multitel, children in Notel caught up to their peers within 2 years after the introduction of TV into their community (Williams, 1986).

EXPERIMENTS INVOLVING
ADOLESCENTS AND YOUNG ADULTS

Laboratory Experiments. Many studies have repeated and extended these findings with children to older age groups. In 1963, Berkowitz conducted a classic series of experiments with college males by using *Champion,* a film about boxing that starred Kirk Douglas. One group of students viewed a scene from the film in which Kirk Douglas is brutally beaten;

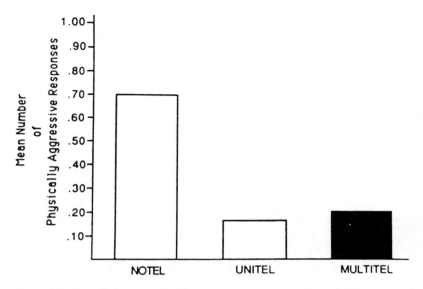

Figure 2.2. Introduction of television into a community that previously had none (Notel) resulted in a significant increase in the mean number of physically aggressive responses among Notel children when compared with children from communities with one TV channel (Unitel) and multiple TV channels (Multitel).

SOURCE: Based on data from Williams (1986). Reproduced from Liebert and Sprafkin, *The early window—Effects of television on children and youth* (3rd ed.). Copyright © 1988 by Allyn and Bacon. Reprinted by permission.

another group viewed a (nonviolent) track meet. In addition, an experimental assistant—named either "Bob" or "*Kirk*" Anderson—angered some of the subjects beforehand. Berkowitz correctly predicted that aggression (as measured by the willingness to give electric shocks to the assistant) would be triggered when the subjects were angered, when they felt that the movie beating was justified, and when the target for their aggression was related in some way to the film (Berkowitz & Geen, 1966, 1967; Berkowitz & Rawlings, 1963).

Later experiments examined the effect of varying the film characters' motives on the students' behavior (Berkowitz & Alioto, 1973; Geen & Stoner, 1972). For example, boxers or football teams were described as engaging in either an athletic contest or a grudge match in which their goal was to injure their opponents. Because males are such heavy consumers of TV sports, these experiments seem pertinent to real life. Interestingly, a link between vengeful motives and greater aggressiveness appeared only in the angered subjects. Among nonangered subjects, the athletic contest condition evoked greater aggression. Dozens of similar experiments exist with similar results (Comstock & Strasburger, 1990).

Field Experiments. Although lab experiments provide convincing data, they may be detecting outcomes that would not occur in everyday life. The most plausible solution to this seems to be the use of naturalistic settings to study subjects—*field* experiments. But such studies also have shortcomings for a completely opposite reason: The "field" is too difficult to manipulate experimentally. Thus several field experiments involving adolescents or young adults (Feshbach & Singer, 1971; Leyens & Camino, 1974; Leyens, Camino, Parke, & Berkowitz, 1975; Loye, Gorney, & Steele, 1977; Milgram & Shotland, 1973) are not only mixed in their outcomes but are unconvincing in their support of the laboratory findings (Gadow & Sprafkin, 1989; Singer, 1989). However, a recent meta-analysis of 28 field studies between 1956 and 1988 concluded that media violence does increase children's and adolescents' aggressive behavior (Wood, Wong, & Chachere, 1991).

Correlational Studies. In the 1970s, a number of investigators surveyed large populations of children and teenagers and tried to determine if heavy TV viewers were also more aggressive. Their findings were remarkably consistent:

1. A survey of 2,300 junior and senior high school students in Maryland asked each student to list their four favorite programs, which were then analyzed for their violent content (McIntyre & Teevan, 1972). Measures of aggression were compiled from a self-reported checklist of activities by using five scales that ranged from aggressive acts (e.g., fighting at school) to serious delinquency (involvement with the law). The greater the aggressiveness or deviancy in behavior, the higher the violent content of their favorite shows.

2. Similarly, a 1972 national sample of 1,500 19-year-old males found that youngsters who expressed a preference for violent programming were significantly more aggressive in their self-reported behavior (although other factors were found to be important as well—e.g., mother's educational level, race, previous behavior) (Robinson & Bachman, 1972). The researchers concluded that TV violence may reinforce or facilitate aggression in teenagers who are already predisposed toward it.

3. Dominick and Greenberg studied 434 male 4th through 6th graders in Michigan and found a positive correlation between high exposure to TV violence and the students' approval of violence and willingness to use it themselves (Dominick & Greenberg, 1972). They reported similar findings in young girls. The greater the exposure to TV violence, the more the students perceived violence as an effective solution to conflict and a personal option for themselves.

4. A combined Maryland/Wisconsin study of more than 600 adolescents attempted to make finer correlations by doing a content analysis of 65 primetime programs and inquiring about theoretical as well as actual situations in which aggression might be used (McLeod, Atkin, & Chaffee, 1972a, 1972b). The measures of aggression included such behaviors as name-calling as well as fighting and were obtained by self-report and peer ratings. The researchers documented a modest positive association, even when variables that could explain both violence exposure and aggression (intelligence, school achievement, socioeconomic status, earlier TV viewing habits) were controlled.

In London, Belson (1978) performed a study of more than 1,500 males aged 12 to 17 years. The representativeness of his sample and his meticulous measures of TV exposure and aggressive behavior made this an elegant study, despite the fact that CBS originally had commissioned the work. Belson examined 13 different types of violence, including "realistic fiction," "horrific," and "in good cause," in addition to different program genres such as cartoons, sports, science fiction, and slapstick (Belson, 1978). By statistically matching his respondents on all variables except those of principal interest, he found:

- Males who viewed large amounts of violent TV committed a much greater number of seriously harmful antisocial and criminal acts than matched peers who were light viewers.
- Less serious categories of aggressive behavior were also positively associated with greater TV violence exposure.
- Other media—newspapers, comic books, films—were also faithful to this pattern.
- Two specific behaviors—aggressiveness in sports and use of foul language—were associated with higher TV exposure.
- Exposure to TV violence produced a higher *quantity* of less serious aggression but its association with the most serious forms of aggression was more *impressive*.

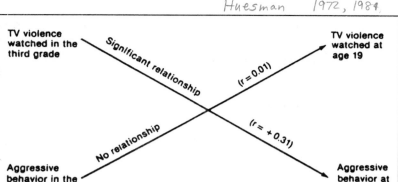

Figure 2.3. Does TV Violence Watched in the Third Grade Correlate With Aggressive Behavior at Age 19? Yes, According to the Results From a Remarkable 10-Year Longitudinal Study.

SOURCE: Liebert and Sprafkin, *The early window—Effects of television on children and youth* (3rd ed.). Copyright © 1988 by Allyn and Bacon. Reprinted by permission.

Longitudinal Studies. As pointed out by Singer (1989), whether contrived experiments are conducted in the laboratory or in the field, they still cannot assess the most crucial linkage: the cumulative effects of TV viewing over an extended period of time. The last 2 decades have seen the evolution of the longitudinal study—field surveys conducted over at least a year's time, which not only establish correlations but produce a strong case for *causality* as well. Six such studies exist, and five unequivocally point to a strong connection between TV violence and aggressive behavior (Huesmann & Eron, 1986; Huesmann, Eron, Lefkowitz, & Walder, 1984; Lefkowitz, Eron, Walder, & Huesmann, 1972; Milavsky, Kessler, Stipp, & Rubens, 1982; Singer et al., 1984; Singer & Singer, 1981).

Three unique studies by Huesmann and his colleagues, reported in 1972, 1984, and 1986, involving children and adolescents represent one of the most extensive and remarkable investigations in the literature (Huesmann et al., 1984; Huesmann & Eron, 1986; Lefkowitz et al., 1972). Using data from a 1963 study of 875 third graders in upstate New York, researchers restudied 460 of the original sample at age 19. The "chicken-and-egg" quandary was thoroughly explored: The relationship between viewing TV violence in the third grade and aggressive behavior 10 years later was highly significant, although aggressive behavior in the third grade was *not* predictive of violent TV consumption at age 19. In 1983, these researchers restudied the original 1963 population, now age 30, and once again found a link between exposure to TV violence at age 8 and aggressive or antisocial behavior, including actual criminal behavior, 22 years later. Their conclusion neatly summarizes the research on media violence:

> Aggressive habits seem to be learned early in life, and once established, are resistant to change and predictive of serious adult antisocial behavior. If a child's observation of media violence promotes the learning of aggressive habits, it can have harmful lifelong consequences. (Huesmann, 1986, p. 129)

A year later, Huesmann and Eron (1986) studied more than 1,000 children in the United States, Australia, Finland, Israel, the Netherlands, and Poland over a 3-year time period. For boys in all countries and for girls in the United States, TV violence was associated with more aggressive behavior and was cumulative over time. Aggressive boys seemed to identify with violent characters, whereas aggressive girls preferred male activities.

META-ANALYSES

Meta-analyses are assessments of research studies in which each study becomes a data point in a new, combined "super study" (Mullen, 1989). Three such studies exist. One analyzes 67 experiments involving about 30,000 subjects (Andison, 1977); one covers 230 studies involving almost 100,000 subjects (Hearold, 1986); and one incorporates 188 studies (Paik, 1991). All support the finding that exposure to TV violence increases the likelihood of subsequent aggressive or antisocial behavior. In addition, Paik (1991) found a dozen studies in which burglary, theft, and criminal violence could be linked with exposure to media violence. Not only was the association statistically significant, but it was also strong enough that dozens of studies with contrary results would have to be done to reverse the finding. In other words, in the meta-analyst's jargon, the numbers are "fail-safe" (Mullen, 1989).

DESENSITIZATION

One particularly alarming aspect of media violence is the possibility that as the amount of entertainment violence increases in TV programs, movies, and rock songs, people are becoming increasingly desensitized to real-life violence. In many laboratory animal experiments, repeated exposure leads to less physiological arousal (Cline, Croft, & Courrier, 1973). If humans were less aroused by repeated exposure to media violence, it might mean that they were becoming desensitized; but shouldn't it also decrease the chance that young people would imitate what they view?

Unfortunately, the answer is no. Exposure to entertainment violence does make young people more indifferent to the plight of others. But it also arouses them *more*, thus *increasing* the chance of aggressive behavior (Thomas, Horton, Lippencott, & Drabman, 1977). For example, young children exposed to a violent TV sequence were less ready to intervene when other children fought or vandalized property (Singer & Singer, 1980). After exposure to a series of "slasher" films depicting gory violence against women, male college students were less sympathetic toward an alleged rape victim and more inclined to hold her responsible (McIntyre & Teevan, 1972; Savitsky et al., 1971). Desensitization to media violence by repeated exposure is particularly apparent (Savitsky et al., 1971) and may be responsible for greater public acceptance of continued high levels of violence in TV programming and movies.

IMPLICATIONS
OF THE RESEARCH

Taken as a whole, this massive body of research on media violence points to four important dimensions in programming: (a) Is the violence rewarded or punished? (b) Is it justified or without any consequences? (c) Is it pertinent to the viewer? (d) Is the viewer susceptible to it? Whatever heightens these four conditions will increase the likelihood that these experiences will help determine future behavior.

How the four basic dimensions influence behavior will depend on the particular portrayal *and* the individual viewer. Certainly, *comprehension* of the adverse consequences of violence, which typically increases with age, might be one inhibiting factor. However, working against this is a popular theme in TV entertainment—the glorification of bravado. *Justified aggression*—especially against women when there is often an erotic undertone—is a powerful facilitator of violence at any age. TV supplies numerous instances in which aggressive and antisocial behavior is *immediately rewarded*, with both the characters and the viewer highly gratified. Finally, it is important to note that lab experiments and surveys investigate the *circumstances* under which aggression can be activated, even if such behavior is rare. Such experiments examine factors that are difficult to disentangle from the everyday flow of experience and, by doing so, permit an important causal inference to be made about TV violence and aggressive behavior. Huesmann's surveys are particularly important here because they document that early exposure to TV violence has a consistent association with aggressive behavior 10 and 20 years later.

In 1964, the Surgeon General's report on smoking established five criteria for causality (U.S. Department of Health, Education, and Welfare, 1964):

1. Temporal relationship between the variables
2. Consistency of the association (replicability)
3. Strength of the association
4. Specificity of the association
5. A coherent explanation that can account for the findings

Television violence meets all of these criteria as *one cause* of child and adolescent aggression (Dietz & Strasburger, 1991; Sege & Dietz, 1994). As one well-known Hollywood producer recently stated:

> I'd be lying if I said that people don't imitate what they see on the screen. I would be a moron to say they don't, because look how dress styles change. We have people who want to look like Julia Roberts and Michelle Pfeiffer and Madonna. Of course we imitate. It would be impossible for me to think they would imitate our dress, our music, our look, but not imitate any of our violence or our other actions. (Auletta). Reprinted by permission; © Ken Auletla. *sic* Originally in *The New Yorker.*

JAPAN VERSUS THE UNITED STATES: CROSS-CULTURAL COMPARISONS

The only country in the world with nearly as much entertainment violence as the United States is Japan. Yet Japanese society is far less violent than American society. If media violence contributes to real-life violence, why isn't Japanese society more affected? A 1981 study (Iwao, Pool, & Hagiwara, 1981) found that the nature of the portrayal of violence is different in Japan: The violence is more realistic and there is a greater emphasis on physical suffering (i.e., the consequences of violence are emphasized). Interestingly, in Japan the "bad guys" commit most of the violence, with the "good guys" suffering the consequences—the exact opposite of American programming. In this context, violence is seen as wrong, a villainous activity with real and painful consequences, rather than as justifiable (Federman, 1993).

TABLE 2.2 Handguns and American Children

- Firearms rank as the second-leading cause of fatal injuries in the United States (33,000 deaths annually). Other countries have relatively few such deaths.
- Each year, the United States has more than 10,000 handgun homicides, compared to 52 or fewer in other developed countries.
- In addition, there are more than 150,000 nonfatal firearm injuries per year.
- The proportion of gun owners in different regions of the United States parallels the percentage of homicides involving firearms and the suicide rate.
- Guns are six times more likely to kill or injure a member of the owner's household than an intruding criminal.
- Toy guns cause more than 1,500 injuries per year.
- The sale of toy guns represents a nearly $100 million industry.
- Weapons appear an average of nine times per hour in primetime TV programs.

SOURCE: Data from Christoffel and Christoffel (1986); Schetky (1985). Reprinted with permission.

GUNS AND THE MEDIA

One of the most urgent public health aspects of entertainment violence is its glorification of guns. Firearms now play a leading role in mortality and morbidity among American youth (American Academy of Pediatrics, 1992). The United States seems to have had a long-standing love affair with guns, and this passion is frequently played out on primetime television and in the movies. Yet the United States leads the Western world in both handgun availability and handgun deaths (Fingerhut & Kleinman, 1990). Firearms are responsible for three fourths of all homicides in the United States, compared with less than one fourth in other countries (Fingerhut & Kleinman, 1990). In 1990, nearly 4,200 teenagers were killed by firearms ("Teen Deaths From Guns," 1993). The United States is "the most heavily armed nation on earth" (Davidson, 1993), with nearly as many firearms as people. Half of all households contain at least one gun (Christoffel, 1991). As a result, American children are more likely to be shot than children in any other country, and guns kept at home are *far more likely* to kill or injure a family member than an intruding criminal (Centers for Disease Control, 1994a; Kellerman et al., 1993; Rushforth, Hirsch, Ford, & Adelson, 1975). On average, nine children and adolescents die each day from injuries due to firearms—not to mention the fact that 80 adults die daily as well (American Academy of Pediatrics, 1992).

Again, the question arises: Is the prevalence of firearms in the United States and the high mortality and morbidity associated with them mere coincidence or cause-and-effect? Certainly, the 500 accidental deaths among children each year from firearms are no coincidence. Children as young as ages 1 to 2 see guns demonstrated in such cartoon shows as *G. I. Joe, He-Man and the Masters of the Universe,* and *Rambo,* and in primetime cop shows. In a New Mexico study, 25 unintentional firearm deaths and 200 woundings were identified within a 4-year period, mostly involving children playing with loaded guns at home (Martin, Sklar, & McFeeley, 1991). But in one case, a 7-year-old boy found his parents' unloaded .357 Magnum revolver, located the ammunition for it, loaded the gun, and accidentally killed his 3-year-old sister. Numerous epidemiological studies have also documented that a *direct* relationship exists between the prevalence of firearms at home or in the community and the risk of homicide (Kellerman et al., 1993; Kellerman & Reay, 1986; Loftin, McDowall, Wiersema, & Cottey, 1991), suicide (Brent et al., 1991, 1993; Kellerman et al., 1992; Kellerman & Reay, 1986; Loftin et al., 1991; Sloan, Rivara, Reay, Ferris, & Kellerman, 1990), and accidental injury (Kellerman & Reay, 1986; Martin et al., 1991; Wintemute, Teret, Kraus, Wright, & Bradfield, 1987) for young people. For teen suicide, the odds of a depressed teenager successfully killing himself increase 75-fold if a gun is kept at home (Rosenberg, Mercy, & Houk, 1991).

ADOLESCENT SUICIDE

During the past 3 decades, the suicide rate among teens has quadrupled—coinciding with the "golden age" of TV violence—and now accounts for 8% of all deaths during adolescence (Scanlan, 1993; Shaffer & Fisher, 1981). Suicidal thoughts are alarmingly common among teenagers: In one study, 25% of junior high school students had considered suicide, 5% of them frequently (Hibbard, Brack, Rauch, & Orr, 1988). Given such a high figure and the fact that suicide gestures outnumber successful attempts by 100 to 200 to 1, giving teenagers access to firearms in the home and making them desirable objects on TV seems particularly foolhardy.

Besides glorifying guns, the media—especially television—may also contribute to adolescent suicide through the modeling of undesirable behavior (Phillips, Carstensen, & Paight, 1989). Many studies, in both the United States and Europe, have demonstrated a link between television programming or news reports and an increase in teenage suicide (Gould & Davidson, 1988; Gould & Shaffer, 1986; Gould, Shaffer, & Kleinman, 1988; Phillips & Carstensen, 1986; Shaffer, Garland, Gould, Fisher, & Trautman, 1988). A key factor may be the extent of the susceptible teenager's identification with the suicide victim (Davidson, Rosenberg,

Mercy, Franklin, & Simmons, 1989). On the other hand, because these studies all involve surveys of large populations, it is impossible to know that exposure to media reports of suicide might have affected a *particular* teenager—the so-called "ecological fallacy" (Morganstern, 1982). Thus a few studies have not found any relationship (Baron & Reiss, 1985; Davidson et al., 1989; Phillips & Paight, 1987). One excellent study examined the effect of four made-for-TV movies about suicide and subsequent rates of attempts and completions. There was a consistent increase, even when other known variables were controlled (Gould & Shaffer, 1986). Overall, these studies point to an increased risk of imitative behavior, probably only in certain susceptible teenagers, but such findings certainly reinforce the importance of Bandura's social learning theory.

VIDEO GAMES

September 1993 marked the debut of *Mortal Kombat,* a home video game so bloody that it comes in two different versions—violent but not gory, and violent and unbelievably gory. The difference between the two is that the Sega version has an unpublished but widely known "blood code." In this fantasy martial arts video game, two opponents fight a three-round bout. In the gory version, the winner can "finish" his opponent by decapitating him or ripping his heart out of his chest. Backed by a $10 million advertising campaign, the game is expected to sell more than 2 million copies, grossing more than $100 million for its manufacturers, Super Nintendo Entertainment System and Sega (Weise, 1993). Other current popular video games include:

Night Trap: Vampires attack scantily clad coeds and, if they are not defeated, the monsters drill the coeds through the neck with a power tool.

Lethal Enforcers: Players fire a large pistol, called a "Justifier," at the screen.

Splatterhouse 3: A man wearing a hockey mask uses meat cleavers and knives to try to save his family from flesh-eating monsters.

Terminator 2: The player is armed with a machine gun, a rocket launcher, and a shotgun to blow away threatening androids.

Such content has drawn video games squarely into the debate over entertainment violence, and with good reason. Violence is a major theme of the most popular video games—40 of 47 games, according to one author (Provenzo, 1991). Video games have come a long way since *Pong* made its debut in 1972 (Provenzo, 1991). Playing video games has become a

TABLE 2.3 Adolescents' Favorite Video Games ($N = 357$)

Category	%
Fantasy violence	32
Sports	29
General entertainment	20
Human violence	17
Educational	2

SOURCE: Funk (1993a). Adapted with permission.

favorite pastime of children and adolescents; consequently, this is now a $7 billion per year industry (Horn, 1994). In one survey of 357 seventh- and eighth-grade students, boys spent a weekly average of 4.2 hours and girls 2 hours playing such games—mostly at home rather than at arcades (Funk, 1993a). However, 15 boys in the sample reported playing 15 or more hours in an average week. Half of the favorite games are violent in content—higher if sports games are included (Funk, 1993b).

Compared with TV violence, considerably less is known about the effect of video games on aggressive behavior. Nevertheless, several studies indicate that video games warrant concern (Funk, 1992, 1993b; Jo & Berkowitz, 1994). Three studies of children found that video game play- ing led to increased aggressive behavior during subsequent free play (Cooper & Mackie, 1986; Schutte, Malouff, Post-Gorden, & Rodasta, 1988; Silvern & Williamson, 1987). Other studies have developed more indirect evidence. One researcher found that teenagers' most frequent responses to 22 common arcade games were aggression and hostility (Mehrabian & Wixen, 1986). Another found that the greater the game's violence content, the greater the player's hostility and anxiety (Anderson & Ford, 1987). And one researcher found that teenagers who watch more violent TV shows prefer playing more violent arcade games as well (Dominick, 1984).

Other concerns about video games have centered around their ability to trigger epileptic seizures in certain susceptible children (Graf, Chatrian, Glass, & Knauss, 1994; Maeda et al., 1990); their displacement of other activities, including school work (Creasey & Myers, 1986; Egli & Myers, 1984); and their role in rather trivial musculoskeletal strains (Greene & Asher, 1982). In addition, there is probably a small group of adolescent males who are truly "addicted" to playing (Egli & Myers, 1984; Funk, 1993b). Contrary to popular belief, playing video games does not increase hand-eye coordination skills (Funk, 1993b; Griffith, Voloschin, Gibb, & Bailey, 1983). On the positive side, one study found that game playing is not as passive as previously thought. Playing *Pac Man* increases energy expenditure by about 80%, the equivalent of walking 2 miles per hour (Segal & Dietz, 1991). Two prosocial applications have been discovered as well: Playing video games during chemotherapy can decrease anxiety (Kolko & Rickard-Figueroa, 1985) and can facilitate rehabilitation in upper-limb burn victims (Adriaenssens, Eggermont, Pyck, & Boeckx, 1988).

Nevertheless, the primary concern remains the violent content of video games and the process involved in playing them (Funk, 1992). Critics charge that violent video games reinforce in children the notions that violence is a common aspect of everyday culture and that pleasure is to be gained from inflicting it (Kinder, 1991). Video game violence involves demonstration (modeling), reward (reinforcement), and practice (rehearsal) (Funk, 1993b). It also frequently uses negative stereotypes, particularly of women as being helpless victims, and encourages an "us-against-them" mentality (Provenzo, 1991). At a time when millions of state and federal tax dollars are being spent on violence prevention programs in schools, it seems incongruous that $6 billion a year is being spent on games teaching that compromise does not exist and that conflict can be resolved only by competition, aggression, and death.

CONCLUSION

The literature on media violence is compelling and clear: Aggression is a learned behavior and young children are particularly vulnerable—although they may not display evidence of being affected until they reach adolescence or young adulthood. Given the inherent limitations of communications research, a few occasional departures from a consistent pattern of findings do not render an entire body of evidence inconclusive (Comstock & Strasburger, 1990). Although the data do not point to media violence as the major cause of violence in society, it is certainly a socially significant one that could be changed virtually overnight if the Hollywood industry and TV networks so desired. As one TV critic observes:

> On average, a violent crime is committed [in the United States] every seventeen seconds. The entertainment industry alone cannot be blamed for this, any more than guns alone, and not the people who pull their triggers, can be blamed for gun-related deaths. But the connections are inescapable. If there were fewer guns, fewer people would be shot to death; if there were fewer violent images, fewer people might be moved to seek violent solutions. (Auletta, 1993, p. 46)

3

ADOLESCENT SEXUALITY AND THE MEDIA

Children, if they watched *Dallas,* already have a working familiarity with lust. They learned about impotence from *Donahue.* . . . Soap operas offer daily classes in frigidity, menopause, abortion, infidelity, and loss of appetite. If they've watched more than one made-for-television movie, they know about rape. . . . Parents should probably view television as a blessing; after all, it took television to finally get sex education out of the schools and back in the home, where it belongs. Call it educational TV.

Linda Ellerbee, *And So It Goes—Adventures in Television,* 1986, p. 34

In the absence of widespread, effective sex education at home or in schools, television and other media have become the leading source of sex education in the United States today. This is a rather sad commentary, considering that American media are the most sexually suggestive and irresponsible in the world. On television each year, American children and teenagers view nearly 14,000 sexual references, innuendoes, and behaviors, few of which involve the use of birth control, self-control, abstinence, or responsibility (Harris & Associates, 1988). On 19 primetime shows viewed most often by 9th and 10th graders, just under three sexual references per hour occurred, usually long kisses or unmarried intercourse (Greenberg, Brown, & Buerkel-Rothfuss, 1993). In action adventure series, most of the sex involved either unmarried intercourse or prostitution (Greenberg et al., 1993). This situation contrasts dramatically with the fact that in the 1990s, adolescent sexuality and sexual activity—teen pregnancy, AIDS and other sexually transmitted diseases (STDs), and abortion—have all become battlegrounds in the public health and political arenas. With one million teen pregnancies a year, and with the highest rate of STDs occurring among adolescents, the United States leads all Western nations in such statistics

(Jones, Forrest, Henshaw, Silverman, & Torres, 1988; Schydlower & Shafer, 1990). By age 17 approximately two thirds of males and one half of females have begun having sexual intercourse (Braverman & Strasburger, 1993). And a sexually active American teenager has a 1 in 6 chance of contracting an STD (Center for Population Options, 1993).

What is meant by content that is sexually suggestive? A few examples will suffice. In 1989, CBS launched *Live-In,* a new situation comedy about a middle-class New Jersey family who imports an Australian *au pair* girl. Tom Shales (1989), a prominent TV critic, reviewed the show:

> By an unwritten law of television, domestic sitcoms must have a randy, hyperglandular teen-age boy in the house. In this case, the kid's name is Danny. . . . When Danny is not salivating or making suggestive remarks, a moronic friend called Gator does it for him.
>
> "So, did you boff her yet?" Gator asked on the first show. When Danny said he hadn't made it to first base, Gator scoffed, "The chick is obviously frigid." Seeing Lisa "naked" then became the project *du jour;* the boys drilled a hole in a wall so they could watch her undress.
>
> As irony will have it, Lisa looked through the hole and saw Danny naked instead. Later, she made mocking reference to his genitals, summoning the image of a baby carrot and remarking, "Immature things are usually small." This was in front of the rest of the family at the dinner table.
>
> Good clean fun? Or puerile pap?

The show aired at 8 p.m. (EDT)—a prime viewing time for most young people—and was viewed in approximately 12.6 million American households.

More recently, FOX Network has created a "Sunday night sleaze parade," according to Shales (1993). *Martin,* a sitcom popular with young blacks, has an episode in which Martin and his girlfriend have a contest to see who can go without sex for 2 weeks without giving in. Then *Living Single,* a sitcom about four women sharing an apartment, deals with the topic of finding men: One of the women is about to go on her first date in 6 months. Her roommate remarks, "I would slide down the banister at city hall." Another one remarks, "No butt, no date." At some point, the women also discuss going to see a movie but then decide there is no point in seeing a film in which Denzel Washington "keeps his shirt on." Queen Latifah, a rap artist and the star of the show, then suggests, "Let's see the new Wesley Snipes movie. I hear there's much nipple" (Shales, 1993).

Even *Grace Under Fire,* an ABC sitcom that was consistently in the top 10 during the 1993-1994 season, succumbed to sexual innuendoes all too often. When her coworkers wonder what to call her, Brett Butler's character suggests that they refer to her as a "throbbing mattress kitten." One older coworker slips and calls her a girl. "I'm 35 years old," she responds. "I've got three kids; I can hide a can of cat food under each breast. If Pops thinks I look like a girl, it makes me *happy*."

BACKGROUND

In 1976, the NBC Standards and Practices department (the network censors) refused to let writer Dan Wakefield use the word "responsible" when "James at 15" and his girlfriend were about to have sexual intercourse for the first time and wanted to discuss birth control (Wakefield, 1987, p. 4). To date, the networks still reject public service announcements (PSAs) and advertisements about contraception, fearing that they would offend some unknown but vocal population in America's hinterland (Quigley, 1987). Recently, only ABC has aired "America Responds to AIDS"—pub-lic service announcements that mention condoms—but only on late-night TV (Painter, 1994). Sex (the commercial networks seem to be telling us) is good for selling everything from shampoo, office machinery, hotel rooms, and beer during primetime series and made-for-TV movies, but a product that would prevent the tragedy of teenage pregnancy—the dreaded "c-word"—must never darken television screens in the United States. Other media have become increasingly sexually explicit as well, particu-larly in the last 2 decades, without much regard for discussing either contra-ception or STDs. Only AIDS has begun to threaten the conspiracy of silence about the health consequences of sexual activity, freeing up the flow of useful and factual information to teenagers, who need it the most.

Why and how has this paradox occurred, and what effect does it have on teenage sexual activity? As with violence, the rates of sexual activity among young people have increased dramatically in the past 2 decades (Braverman & Strasburger, 1993). At the same time, the amount of sexual suggestiveness in the media has increased dramatically as well. Although the data are not as convincing as with media violence, a number of studies show that media sex still warrants considerable concern.

TELEVISION AS A SOURCE
OF SEXUAL INFORMATION

In any given society, at any given moment in history, people become sexual the same way they become anything else. Without much reflection they pick up

> directions from their social environment. They acquire and assemble meanings, skills and values from the people around them. Critical choices are often made by going along and drifting. People learn when they are quite young the few things they are expected to be, and continue slowly to accumulate a belief in who they are and ought to be throughout the rest of childhood, adolescence, and adulthood.
>
> John Gagnon, social science
> researcher (Roberts, 1983, p. 9)

Content analyses can determine what is being shown on television, but they do not reveal what teenagers actually *learn* from these portrayals. Apart from its pervasiveness, accessibility, and content, television is an effective sex educator for several other reasons (Haffner & Kelly, 1987). Alternative sex educators, such as parents, may supply only restricted or biased information (Pearl, Bouthilet, & Lazar, 1982). They rarely discuss sexual activity or birth control, making a majority of teenagers dissatisfied with their parents' educational efforts (Selverstone, 1992). Sex education programs in school may also have a limited impact on adolescents: Only 10% to 30% of schools offer comprehensive, high-quality programs; gains in knowledge may be small; and many curricula begin after teenagers have already begun having intercourse (Dawson, 1986; Furstenberg, Moore, & Peterson, 1985; Harris & Associates, 1986; Kirby, 1980; Marsiglio & Mott, 1986; Selverstone, 1992; Zelnik & Kim, 1982). Although their counsel is frequently sought, peers may also play a limited role in sex education because the information they offer may be incomplete, misleading, distorted, and transmitted by means of jokes or boasting, and may, in fact, be influenced by the media as well (Coles & Stokes, 1985).

When teenagers or adults are asked about the influence of television, they acknowledge its central role. A 1981 study of adolescents' sources of information found that the media ranked just behind peers in importance (Thornburg, 1981). The landmark National Institute of Mental Health report on television in 1982 noted that American teenagers rate the media third, behind peers and parents, as major influences on their attitudes and behavior (Pearl et al., 1982). A 1987 Harris report, which surveyed 1,250 adults nationwide, found that more than 80% of adults feel that TV is a major influence on teenagers' values and behavior (Harris & Associates, 1987). Most parents believe that television is the second most important source of information—after themselves—and a 1986 Harris report, which surveyed 1,000 teenagers nationwide, seems to support parents' notion that they are "number one" (Harris & Associates, 1986; Sexuality Study Group, 1990). Yet when one realizes that friends and even parents may all be greatly influenced themselves by television, the cumulative effects of television may outweigh all other influences.

Not only are the media important generic sources of information, but particular topics may also be far more intensively discussed than elsewhere (Harris & Associates, 1988). For instance, television may be the "medium of choice" for dissemination of information about AIDS (Goldberg, 1987). Of the nearly 2,000 adults surveyed in a 1988 Roper poll, 96% said they had heard a report on AIDS in the last 3 months on TV, and 73% thought that TV was doing an effective job of educating the public (Jones, 1988).

WHAT DO TEENAGERS
LEARN FROM TELEVISION?

Many studies have documented television's ability to transmit information and to shape attitudes. Television influences viewers' perceptions of social behavior and social reality (Bandura, 1977; Hawkins & Pingree, 1982), contributes to cultural norms (Gerbner, 1985; Greenberg, 1982), and conveys messages concerning the behaviors it portrays (Bandura, 1977; Roberts, 1982). Television may offer teenagers "scripts" for sexual behavior that they might not be able to observe anywhere else (Gagnon & Simon, 1987; Silverman-Watkins, 1983).

It is well-known that teenagers sometimes resemble actors and actresses as they experiment with different facets of their newly forming identities and try on different social "masks." In particular, the idiosyncrasies of adolescent psychology seem to combine to conspire against successful use of contraception during early and middle adolescence (Strasburger & Brown, 1991). Teenagers often see themselves egocentrically as actors in their own "personal fable" (Elkind, 1993, p. 72), in which the normal rules (e.g., having unprotected sexual intercourse may lead to pregnancy) are suspended—exactly as on television. Even though 70% of teenagers by age 16 have reached the final level of cognitive operational thinking described by Piaget (1972)—sequential logical thinking (formal operations)—they may still suffer from what Elkind calls "pseudostupidity": "The capacity to conceive many different alternatives is not immediately coupled with the ability to assign priorities and to decide which choice is more or less appropriate than others" (Elkind, 1984, p. 384). One major conclusion of the 1985 Guttmacher report, which found that the United States has the highest rate of teenage pregnancy among 37 developed

TABLE 3.1 Teenagers' Versus Adults' Perceptions of Sex on Television[a]

Yes, TV Gives a Realistic Picture About	Teenagers (N = 1,000)	Adults (N = 1,253)
Sexually transmitted diseases	45	28
Pregnancy	41	24
Birth control	28	17
People making love	24	18

SOUCE: Adapted from Harris and Associates (1986).
[a] Values are represented in percentages.

countries (despite the fact that American teenagers are no more sexually active than French, Canadian, or Belgian teens), concerned the media:

> American teenagers seem to have inherited the worst of all possible worlds regarding their exposure to messages about sex: Movies, music, radio and TV tell them that sex is romantic, exciting, titillating; premarital sex and co-habitation are visible ways of life among adults they see and hear about. . . . Yet, at the same time, young people get the message good girls should say no. Almost nothing they see or hear about sex informs them about contraception or the importance of avoiding pregnancy. For example, they are more likely to hear about abortions than about contraception on the daily TV soap opera. Such messages lead to an ambivalence about sex that stifles communication and exposes young people to increased risk of pregnancy, out-of-wedlock births, and abortions. (Jones et al., 1985, p. 61)

Given the content of current American television, one expects that heavy viewers would believe that premarital sex, extramarital sex, rape, and prostitution are all more common than they really are (Greenberg, 1994). Although teenagers are probably not as susceptible as young children to media violence, they may be more susceptible to sexual content. Indeed, they often believe that what they watch on television is real (Harris & Associates, 1986). This belief is actually highest among heavier consumers of TV and among adolescent populations with the highest teenage pregnancy rates (Harris & Associates, 1985; see Table 3.1). Regular exposure to sexy TV might alter teenagers' self-perceptions as well. They might be less satisfied with their own sex lives or have higher expectations of their prospective partners (Greenberg, 1994).

If, as Gerbner states, "daytime serials comprise the most prolific single source of medical advice in America" (Gerbner, Morgan, & Signorielli, 1982, p. 295), then teenagers, particularly females, are getting bad advice.

One of the main messages from the soaps is that adults do not use contraception and, in fact, do not plan for sex at all. Being "swept away" is the natural way to have sex (Wattleton, 1987). Unfortunately, this message dovetails with adolescents' own ambivalence about sex and helps to explain that the leading reasons sexually active teens give for not using contraception are that sex "just happens" and there was "no time to prepare" (Harris & Associates, 1986). Teenagers already overestimate the number of their peers who are engaging in sexual intercourse (Zabin, Hirsch, Smith, & Hardy, 1984). In one survey, teenagers reported that TV was equally or more encouraging about sex than either their best male or female friends (Brown & Newcomer, 1991). In this sense, television may function as a kind of "super peer." Heavy doses of television may accentuate their feelings that everyone is "doing it" except them and may contribute to the gradual but steadily decreasing age when both males and females first have intercourse that has been occurring during the past 2 decades (Braverman & Strasburger, 1993).

Several studies support these speculations. When college students were asked to identify models of responsible and irresponsible sexual behavior, they selected primarily media figures (Fabes & Strouse, 1984). And those who selected media figures as models of sexual *responsibility* had more permissive sexual attitudes and higher rates of sexual activity themselves (Fabes & Strouse, 1987). College students who were heavy viewers of soap operas estimated higher percentages of people in the real world who are divorced or have illegitimate children than did light viewers (Buerkel-Rothfuss & Mayes, 1981; Carveth & Alexander, 1985). In one study, pregnant teenagers were twice as likely to think that TV relationships are like real-life relationships than nonpregnant teenagers and that TV characters would not use contraception if involved in a sexual relationship (Corder-Bolz, 1981). And adolescents who identify closely with TV personalities and think that their TV role models are more proficient at sex than they are, or who think that TV sexual portrayals are accurate, report being *less* satisfied with their status as virgins or with their own intercourse experiences (Baran, 1976a, 1976b; Courtright & Baran, 1980).

Studies show that subtler aspects of human sexuality may also be affected (Signorielli, 1993). For example, young children who watch 25 hours or more of TV demonstrated more stereotypical sex role attitudes than those who watched 10 hours or less per week (Freuh & McGhee, 1975). The heavy viewers thought that boys should play with guns and trucks, but girls should play with dolls. Numerous studies have shown that television cultivates such notions as "women are happiest at home raising children" and "men are born with more ambition than women," particularly among heavy viewers (Morgan, 1987). Even Saturday morning cartoons contribute to this traditional view of girls and women (Canonzoneri, 1984). As the National Institute of Mental Health report concluded in 1982, the single most significant aspect of a child's learning about sex is the set of messages that relate to "normal" male and female characteristics and roles in life (Roberts, 1982). Although television has made some progress in this area—for instance, males currently outnumber females 2 to 1 instead of 3 to 1 in the 1970s (Gerbner, 1993)—even the independent women shown in current programming frequently depend on men for advice and direction, lose control more often than men, and become more emotionally involved. This has led one critic to charge that the traditional female roles are merely being "dished up in new guises" (Canonzoneri, 1984, p. 15).

MOVIES

As a medium, movies are less significant than television because they see p. 21 command much less time from the average teenager and are usually viewed with friends, thus allowing the process of socialization to temper whatever potential effects may exist. If teenagers see two movies per week at their local cinema, that still represents only 10% to 15% of the time they spend watching television in an average week. This does not imply that movies are insignificant, however. The widespread prevalence of VCRs—77% of American households have one (Nielsen Media Research, 1993)—makes the local video store a far more important consideration than the cinema.

In a survey of 15- and 16-year-olds in three Michigan cities, more than half had seen the majority of the most popular R-rated movies between 1982 and 1984 either in cinemas or on videocassette (Greenberg et al., 1986). Compared with primetime television, these movies have seven times more sexual acts or references, which are depicted much more explicitly (Greenberg et al., 1993). The ratio of unmarried to married intercourse is 32 to 1. As Greenberg (1994) notes, "What television suggests, movies and videos do" (p. 180). Content analyses of the most popular movies of 1959, 1969, and 1979 demonstrate the trend toward increasing explicitness in depictions of sexual themes, but the themes themselves have remained stable: Sex is for the young and is an "action activity" rather than a means of expressing affection (Abramson & Mechanic, 1983). And, as on TV, intercourse and contraception are distant cousins, at best.

The years between 1970 and 1989 represented an era of teenage "sexploitation" films. Hollywood pandered to the adolescent population, presumably because of demographic considerations: Teenagers comprise the largest movie-going segment of the population. Such movies as *Porky's I-III, The Last American Virgin, Going All the Way, The First Time, Endless Love, Risky Business, Bachelor Party,* and *Fast Times at Ridgemont High* have dealt with teenage sex. Although parents may complain about their teenagers' interest in such films, the adults making films in Hollywood (and the adult cinema operators allowing underage teenagers to see R-rated films) are the ones who are ultimately responsible.

PRINT MEDIA

Contemporary magazines reflect the same trend as seen in television and movies—a shift away from naive or innocent romantic love in the 1950s and 1960s (e.g., *Bachelor Father* and *My Little Margie* on TV; *Beach Blanket Bingo* and *Love Me Tender* in the movies) to increasingly clinical concerns about sexual functioning. Content analyses demonstrate that by the 1970s, such mainstream magazines as *Ladies Home Journal, Good Housekeeping, McCall's,* and *Time* contained a three-fold increase in the number of articles that discussed sexual functioning and a six-fold increase in sexual terms used (Bailey, 1969; Herold & Foster, 1975; Scott, 1986). Accompanying this change was a shift from discussion of sexual "morality" to a concern about sexual "quality," a skepticism about virginity at marriage, and a liberalized view of extramarital sex (Silverman-Watkins, 1983). However, the print media are also far more likely to discuss contraception and advertise birth control products. In the only study of the print media that adolescents read, Klein et al. (1993) found that *Seventeen, Sports Illustrated, Teen, Time, Ebony, Young Miss, Jet, Newsweek,* and *Vogue* accounted for more than half of all reported reading (the survey was conducted before *Sassy* was introduced). Adolescents who read sports or music magazines were more likely to report engaging in risky behaviors. A separate content analysis of *Seventeen* and *Sassy* revealed that most of the stories in these two popular magazines contain very traditional socialization messages for girls, including depending on someone else to solve one's personal problems (Peirce, 1993).

THE NATURE OF THE RESEARCH

Unlike the violence research, studies of the impact of sexy television and movies are, by necessity, considerably scarcer and more limited. Researchers cannot simply show a group of 13-year-olds several X-rated movies and then measure the attitudinal or behavioral changes that result. But a number of research modalities have yielded important data.

Content Analyses. These studies simply assay the amount of sexual material in current programming without addressing causality. In the 1980s, content analyses have found that:

- Americans view more than 27 instances per hour of sexual behavior (Harris & Associates, 1988).
- Annually, the networks transmit approximately 65,000 instances of sexual material per year during the afternoon and primetime periods alone (Harris & Associates, 1988). The average American child or teenager views nearly 14,000 sexual references, innuendoes, and behaviors each year, yet less than 150 involve birth control, abstinence, STDs, or responsibility (Harris & Associates, 1988).
- The sexual content of soap operas has more than doubled since 1980 (Greenberg et al., 1986). Soap opera sex is 24 times more common between unmarried partners than between spouses, and birth control is rarely mentioned (Lowry & Towles, 1989).
- From 1975 to 1988, the amount of sexual behaviors on primetime television doubled, the amount of suggestiveness increased more than four-fold, and sexual intercourse was portrayed for the first time (Harris & Associates, 1988).
- Seventy-five percent of MTV videos that tell a story ("concept videos") involve sexual imagery, more than half involve violence, and 80% of the time the two are combined: violence against women (Sherman & Dominick, 1986).
- Movies have become increasingly explicit in depicting sexual themes (Greenberg et al., 1987).
- Rock music has become increasingly graphic as well (Brown & Hendee, 1989; Prinsky & Rosenbaum, 1987).

Most researchers would agree that soap operas represent the most sensational, inaccurate, and addictive view of adult sexuality. Extramarital sex is portrayed eight times more commonly than sex between spouses; 94% of the sexual encounters depicted are between people not married to each other (Greenberg, Abelman, & Neuendorf, 1981). Sex is frequently portrayed as being impersonal, emotionless, and exploitative (Sprafkin &

Silverman, 1982). Despite the fact that the mention or use of contraception is extremely rare, women seldom get pregnant; no one ever gets an STD unless he or she is a prostitute or gay (Greenberg, Abelman, & Neuendorf, 1981). Homosexuals are rarely portrayed or are stereotyped as victims or villains (Lowry, Love, & Kirby, 1987). Unfortunately, teenage females are particularly avid viewers of afternoon soap operas, and the sexiest soaps, *All My Children* and *General Hospital,* also command the largest teenage audience (Greenberg, 1994; Lowry et al., 1987). The former contains 5.2 sex references per hour, the latter 3.1; and most of the time these involve discussions of intercourse (Greenberg, 1994). Soaps particularly popular with teenagers have increased their sexual content by 21% since 1982 and by 103% since 1980 (Greenberg, 1994).

If advertisements had been counted in the longitudinal studies of content, the results would have been even higher. From the time the Noxema girl advised male viewers to "take it off, take it all off," to Brooke Shields's "nothing comes between me and my Calvins," to present-day ads for beer, wine coolers, and perfume, advertising has always used explicit visual imagery to try to make a sale (Kilbourne, 1993). Teenage girls spend an estimated $5 billion a year on cosmetics alone (Graham & Hamdan, 1987). By 1977, one researcher found that nearly one third of all advertisements on primetime TV "used as selling points the desirability of sex appeal, youth, or beauty, and/or those in which sex appeal (physical attractiveness) of commercial actors or actresses was a selling point" (Tan, 1979, p. 285). One byproduct of the feminist movement of the 1970s has been that men are now being increasingly exploited for their sex appeal the way women once were (Svetkey, 1994). American media have become equal-opportunity exploiters.

In the 1990s, advertisers now seem to be wrestling with the images of both sexes. A recent series of advertisements show women with "attitude" (Leo, 1993, p. A11). For example, a Bodyslimmers ad that shows a woman wearing a one-piece undergarment reads: "While you don't necessarily dress for men, it doesn't hurt, on occasion, to see one drool like the pathetic dog that he is." A TV car ad has two women discussing whether men buy big cars because they are worried about the size of their penises: "He must be overcompensating for a . . . shortcoming?" says one. Then a handsome man drives up in a Hyundai Elantra, and her friend says, "I wonder what he's got under the hood" (Leo, 1993).

Correlational Studies. Clearly, according to content analyses, American television is both sexy and suggestive. Simple common sense would tell us that this is not healthy for children and younger adolescents. But some people want stronger evidence. Does all of this sexy content actually *harm* children, or is it merely fantasy and entertainment? Do teenagers who become sexually active at a younger age do so because of exposure to sexy media, or do they simply prefer to watch such programming? Unfortunately, correlational studies are rare. Only four studies exist that have tried to assess the relationship between early onset of sexual intercourse and the amount of sexual content viewed on television. Only one was longitudinal, but all have demonstrated measurable effects:

- In a study of 75 adolescent girls, half pregnant and half nonpregnant, the pregnant girls watched more soap operas before becoming pregnant and were less likely to think that their favorite soap characters would use birth control (Corder-Bolz, 1981). (Soderman, et al, 1988)
- A study of 391 junior high school students in North Carolina found that those who selectively viewed more sexy TV were more likely to have begun having sexual intercourse in the preceding year (Brown & Newcomer, 1991).
- A study of 326 Cleveland teenagers showed that those with a preference for MTV had increased amounts of sexual experience in their mid-teen years (Peterson & Kahn, 1984).
- Data from the National Surveys of Children revealed that males who watched more TV had the highest prevalence of sexual intercourse, and teens who watched TV apart from their family had a rate of intercourse 3 to 6 times higher than those who viewed with their family (Peterson, Moore, & Furstenberg, 1991).

To date, no good longitudinal correlational study links exposure to large amounts of sexy TV or movies with the early onset of sexual intercourse. Such studies exist in other areas of media research—for example, TV violence and aggressive behavior, amount of TV viewed and obesity. There is an urgent need for such a study.

Experimental Studies. Severe constraints exist when studying *any* aspect of childhood or adolescent sexuality. For example, in 1991 U.S. Secretary of Health and Human Services Louis Sullivan canceled a planned 5-year, $18 million survey of 24,000 young people in Grades 7 through 11 because he was worried about the "inadvertent message this survey could send" (Marshall, 1991, p. 502). The survey would have provided valuable information about teenagers' sexual habits and would have included several questions about their media habits as well. Fortunately, the National Institutes of Health decided to fund the project in 1994. Even in the

1990s, researchers are still fighting the old shibboleth that if you ask kids about sex, they will get ideas they would not otherwise have had. Studies have examined the effectiveness of sex in advertising and programming: High school girls shown 15 "beauty commercials" were more likely to believe that physical attractiveness was important for them than were girls shown neutral commercials (Tan, 1979). Male college students who viewed a single episode of *Charlie's Angels* were harsher in their evaluations of the beauty of potential dates than males who had not seen the episode (Kenrick & Guttieres, 1980), and male college students shown centerfolds from *Playboy* and *Penthouse* were more likely to find their own girlfriends less sexually attractive (Weaver, Masland, & Zillmann, 1984).

Studies have also examined the impact of sexual content on attitude formation. For example, college students shown sexually explicit films reported a greater acceptance of sexual infidelity and promiscuity than controls did (Zillmann, 1994), and adolescents viewing only 10 music videos were more likely to agree with the notion that premarital sex is acceptable (Greeson & Williams, 1986). In two studies, college students' disapproval of rape could be lessened by exposure to only 9 minutes of scenes taken from television programs and R-rated movies or viewing 5 hours of sexually explicit films over a 6-week period (Brown, Childers, & Waszak, 1990; Zillmann & Bryant, 1982). Finally, both male and female college students exposed to hour-long nonviolent X-rated videos over a 6-week period reported less satisfaction with their intimate partners (Zillmann & Bryant, 1988). The researchers concluded that "great sexual joy and ecstasy are accessible to parties who just met, who are in no way committed to one another, and who will part shortly, never to meet again" (Zillmann & Bryant, 1988, p. 450)—certainly an ominous finding for those interested in diminishing rates of adolescent sexual intercourse.

Obviously, studying college students is considerably easier than studying younger adolescents, particularly when sexual behavior is the variable being assessed. Although 50% of high school seniors are engaging in sexual intercourse (Braverman & Strasburger, 1993) and adolescents are bombarded with sexual messages in the media, school administrators and parents are still reluctant to have their teenagers questioned about their sexual activities, even with the use of informed consent. Therefore, there is currently a return to small-scale laboratory and field studies, two of which have shown intriguing results. In the first, "massive exposure" to primetime programming that dealt with pre-, extra-, or nonmarital sex desensitized young viewers to such "improprieties." However, several factors mitigated against this: a clearly defined value system within the family, an ability to discuss important issues freely within the family, and active, critical viewing skills (Bryant & Rockwell, 1994). In the second, a small study of adolescents' interpretations of soap operas, Walsh-Childers found that teenagers' own sexual "schemas" influenced their perceptions of the characters' relationships (Walsh-Childers, 1991). Interestingly, the mention of birth control did *not* have to be explicit to be effective. In fact, using the euphemism "protection" seemed to be preferable.

CONTRACEPTIVE ADVERTISING

One of the key findings of the 1985 Guttmacher report was that the United States' high teenage pregnancy rate partially results from inadequate access to birth control information and products (Jones et al., 1988). It seems odd, perhaps even hypocritical, that as American culture has become increasingly "sexualized" in the past 20 years, the one taboo remaining is the public mention of birth control. In 1985, the American College of Obstetrics and Gynecology (ACOG) made headlines when "I Intend," its public service announcement (PSA) about teen pregnancy, was banned from all three major networks. The one offensive line that had to be removed before the networks agreed to run the PSA said, "Unintended pregnancies have risks . . . greater risks than any of today's contraceptives" (Strasburger, 1989a). Network executives claim that such PSAs or advertisements for birth control products would offend many viewers. Yet no evidence supports this assertion. Birth control ads for nonprescription products air on many local TV stations across the United States (e.g., KABC-Los Angeles) without complaints being registered. In addition, the 1987 Harris report shows that a majority of the American public—including 62% of the Catholics surveyed—*favor* birth control advertising on television (Harris & Associates, 1987). On the other hand, the DeMoss Foundation spends more than $100 million per year on its antiabortion "Life, What a Beautiful Choice" public service advertising campaign yet never mentions birth control (Murchek, 1994).

Would advertising condoms and birth control pills have an impact on the rates of teen pregnancy or HIV acquisition? The Guttmacher data (Jones et al., 1988) seem to indicate that the answer is yes for teen pregnancy because European countries have far lower rates of teen pregnancy and far more widespread media discussion and advertising of birth control products. Furthermore, according to Population Services International, when Zaire began advertising condoms, there was a 20-fold

TABLE 3.2   Television and Birth Control[a] (*N* = 1,250 adults)

	Yes	*No*
Should characters on TV shows be shown using birth control?	59	34
Is contraception too controversial to be mentioned on TV shows?	32	64
Are you in favor of advertising birth control on TV?	60	37
Would birth control advertising		
encourage teenagers to have sex?	42	52
encourage teens to use contraceptives?	82	14

SOURCE: Adapted from Harris (1987).
[a] Values are represented in percentages.

increase in the number of condoms sold in just 3 years—from 900,000 in 1988 to 18 million in 1991 (Alter, 1994). In a relevant "natural experiment," in Maryland, Earvin "Magic" Johnson's announcement of his HIV infection was associated with a decline in "one-night stands" and sex with multiple partners in the subsequent 14 weeks (Centers for Disease Control, 1993). It also resulted in increased awareness about AIDS (Kalichman & Hunter, 1992).

Would advertising birth control products make teenagers more sexually active than they already are? *No evidence available indicates that allowing freer access to birth control encourages teenagers to become sexually active at a younger age* (Reichelt, 1978; Strasburger & Brown, 1991). In fact, the data indicate the exact opposite: Teenage females engage in unprotected intercourse for 6 months to 1 year before seeking medical attention for birth control (Zabin et al., 1984). In 1986, the American Academy of Pediatrics joined ACOG in issuing a call for contraceptive advertising on TV in the United States (American Academy of Pediatrics, 1986). Despite the hopes of many public health officials, the fear of AIDS may not be sufficient to increase teenagers' use of contraception. In several longitudinal studies, the use of condoms has actually *decreased* among teenagers and young adults, despite widespread publicity (Kegeles, Adler, & Irwin, 1988; Ku, Sonenstein, & Pleck, 1993). Currently, contraceptive advertising remains banned from national network programming and is subject to the discretion of local station managers. Thus a major potential solution to a significant American health problem is being thwarted by a few very powerful but fearful executives.

PORNOGRAPHY

The relationship of pornography to behavior remains an important health issue as well as a controversial First Amendment issue. Interestingly, print media are protected constitutionally by the First Amendment, whereas broadcast media are subject to regulation under the 1934 FCC charter. To date, cable television remains in a legal netherworld.

Exposure

Teenagers have surprisingly ready access to a variety of R-rated and X-rated material. According to one study, by age 15, 92% of males and 84% of females had seen or read *Playboy* or *Playgirl*, and by age 18, virtually all had (Brown & Bryant, 1989). Exposure to more hard-core magazines began at an average age of 13.5 years, and 92% of 13- to 15-year-olds reported having seen an X-rated film (Brown & Bryant, 1989). Of 16 popular R-rated films, Greenberg et al. (1993) found that 53% to 77% of 9th and 10th graders had seen most of them.

Research

Current research seems to indicate that pornography itself is harmless unless violence is also involved. In that situation, aggression might increase, because there is a known relationship between portrayals of violence and subsequent aggressive behavior (Cline, 1994; Harris, 1994; Huston et al., 1992; Linz & Malamuth, 1993; Lyons, Anderson, & Larson, 1994; Malamuth, 1993; Weaver, 1994). The term *pornography* means different things to different people. The current state-of-the-art subdivides the research according to content (Huston et al., 1992; Malamuth, 1993):

Erotica. R- or X-rated material with implied or actual sexual contact but no violence or coercion. *No antisocial effect* (Donnerstein, Linz, & Penrod, 1987).

X-Rated Material Degrading to Women. Nonviolent, XXX-videos in which women are the eager recipients of any and all male sexual urges. *Highly controversial.* Most studies find no antisocial effect. But some researchers suggest that attitudes may be molded or changed by repeated exposure. In a study of college students, massive doses of pornographic films led to overestimates of uncommon sexual practices, decreased concern about the crime of rape, loss of sympathy for the women's liberation movement, and, among men, a more callous attitude toward sex (Zillmann & Bryant, 1982, 1988).

Violent Pornography. X-rated videos in which the woman victim is shown to be enjoying the assault or rape. *Known antisocial effects.* This is one of the most dangerous types of combinations—sex and violence— although it is probably the violent content that takes priority. Men exposed to such material show increased aggression against women in laboratory studies and increased callousness in their attitudes (Donnerstein, 1984; Linz & Malamuth, 1993). But men exposed to nonsexual violence can show the same effect as well (Huston et al., 1992).

Non-X-Rated Sexual Aggression Against Women. Broadcast or movie programming in which women are depicted as deriving pleasure from sexual abuse or assault. *Probable antisocial effects.* Such content may reinforce callous attitudes toward rape and rape victims.

Sexualized Violence Against Women. R-rated videos that are less sexu- ally explicit but far more violent than X-rated ones, often shown on cable-TV or available in video stores. *Probable antisocial effects.* These do not involve rape but do contain scenes of women being tortured, murdered, or mutilated in a sexual context. This may be the single most important category for teenagers because it is more "mainstream" and represents an important genre of Hollywood "slice 'em and dice 'em" movies (e.g., *Halloween I-V, Nightmare on Elm Street I-V, Friday the 13th I-VIII, Texas Chainsaw Massacre I-II*). Often, the title alone tells the tale: *Hide and Go Shriek, Kiss Daddy Goodbye, Return to Horror High, Slaughter High, The Dorm That Dripped Blood, Chopping Mall, Murderlust, Deadtime Sto- ries, Splatter University, Lady Stay Dead, I Dismember Mama, Watch Me When I Kill, Lunch Meat.*

maybe

Because sex is something that is not usually discussed or observed, except in the media, teenagers who are faithful viewers of such movies may be learning that acting aggressively toward women is expected and normal. Studies show that exposure to such material can result in de- sensitization to sexual violence, for both young men and women (Donnerstein et al., 1987). However, such studies cannot always be replicated (Linz & Donnerstein, 1988; Weaver, 1994). As two prominent researchers note, "Our research suggests that you need not look any further than the family's own television set to find demeaning depictions of women available to far more viewers than pornographic material" (Linz & Donnerstein, 1988, p. 184).

UNANSWERED QUESTIONS

Far more research is needed regarding teenagers' sexual practices, how they make their sexual decisions, and which teenagers are particularly susceptible to media influences. Longitudinal correlational analyses of teenagers' media consumption and their sexual activity are particularly needed. Because the media constantly change, ongoing content analyses are also needed.

Despite this discussion, not all media are unhealthy or irresponsible for young people. Some shows have dealt responsibly with the issues of teenage sexual activity and teenage pregnancy: *Facts of Life, Growing Pains, Blossom, Beverly Hills 90210,* and several others. Made-for-TV movies such as *Babies Having Babies* and *Daddy* have used extremely frank language to good, educational effect. *Cagney and Lacey* contained one of the first instances of a TV mother talking to her *son* about responsibility and birth control. On *St. Elsewhere* the only known mention of a diaphragm on primetime TV was aired during the 1987-1988 season, although it required the user to be the Chief of Obstetrics and Gynecology to accomplish it. But these are the exceptions rather than the rule on American television. And, unfortunately, it has not been the tragedy of teenage pregnancy or the high rates of early adolescent sexual activity that have blunted the red pencil of the network censors but rather the appearance of AIDS as a national health emergency. But here, too, much educational programming may be made possible to benefit teenagers. One example is the 1987-1988 episode of *L.A. Law* that discussed the risk of AIDS in heterosexual intercourse but also included good advice on birth control and choosing sexual partners (see Strasburger, 1989a). However, until the political and funding climate changes, and until adults understand that asking children and teenagers about sex will not provoke them into early sexual activity, we will simply have to speculate about many of these crucial issues.

As one author sadly notes:

> I've often wondered what it would be like if we taught young people swimming the same way we teach sexuality. If we told them that swimming was an important adult activity, one they will all have to be skilled at when they grow up, but we never talked with them about it. We never showed them the

pool. We just allowed them to stand outside closed doors and listen to all the splashing. Occasionally, they might catch a glimpse of partially-clothed people going in and out of the door to the pool and maybe they'd find a hidden book on the art of swimming, but when they asked a question about how swimming felt or what it was about, they would be greeted with blank or embarrassed looks. Suddenly, when they turn 18 we would fling open the doors to the swimming pool and they would jump in. Miraculously, some might learn to tread water, but many would drown. (Roberts, 1983, p. 10)

4

ADOLESCENTS, DRUGS, AND THE MEDIA

If 434,000 Americans were to die in the Persian Gulf war, governments would topple. World War III would be under way. The world and the world order as we know it would be shaken to its foundations. Yet, last week, the Centers for Disease Control announced that 434,000 Americans died in 1988 from tobacco-related causes. The body count drew only a shrug and a few paragraphs of newspaper ink.

J. Beck,
Albuquerque Journal, February 8, 1991
© Associated Press. Reprinted with permission.

Slogans that teach young people to "Say no" to drugs and sex have a nice ring to them. But . . . they are as effective in prevention of adolescent pregnancy and drug abuse as the saying "Have a nice day" is in preventing clinical depression.

Michael Carrera, Ed.D.,
at the hearings of the
Presidential Commission on AIDS

An interesting paradox exists in the American media: Advertisements for condoms and other birth control products—which could prevent untold numbers of teenage pregnancies and sexually transmitted diseases—are forbidden on three of the four major national networks (Quigley, 1987). Yet all four networks frequently advertise products that cause disease and death in thousands of teenagers and adults annually—alcohol and cigarettes. Television is not the sole culprit, however. Of the nearly $4 billion a year that tobacco companies spend on advertising (MacKenzie, Bartecchi, & Schrier, 1994), two thirds goes toward promotional activities (e.g., rock concerts, sports events) and so-called passive or inadvertent advertising—for example, logos at sports arenas or on racing cars (Blum, 1991; Centers for Disease Control, 1990). An analysis of sports programming from 1990

TABLE 4.1 Inadvertent or Passive Advertising of Cigarettes on Television: Exposure of the Marlboro Logo During the 1989 Marlboro Grand Prix Auto Racing Telecast

Type of Exposure	Number of Exposures
Small raceway sign	4,998
Large billboard	519
Marlboro car	249
Other	167
Total number of times Marlboro seen or mentioned	5,933
Total length of broadcast	94 minutes
Total time Marlboro seen	46 minutes[a]
Percentage of time Marlboro seen	49%

SOURCE: Adapted from Blum, A., *N Engl J Med*, 1991; 324:915. © Copyright 1991. *Massachusetts Medical Society*. All rights reserved.
[a] Total value of this commercial exposure was calculated by *Sponsors Report* to be $1,129,340.

to 1992 found that the incidence of passive advertising was 1.5 times per hour overall but that sports car racing contained inadvertent advertising during half of its air time (Madden & Grube, 1994). Despite the 1971 ban on cigarette advertising in the broadcast media, cigarettes remain the most heavily advertised consumer product in the United States (Blum, 1991; Brown & Walsh-Childers, 1994). By comparison, beer and wine manufacturers spend only $2 billion a year (Koenig, 1992), but, again, much of this advertising is considered deceptive—it glorifies the sexiness and desirability of alcohol without depicting any of the real dangers involved in drinking.

Although there is some legitimate controversy about how much of an impact such advertising has on young people and their decisions whether to use cigarettes or alcohol, advertising clearly works. In June 1994 alone, advertisers purchased about $4 billion in "up-front" air time for the fall season in less than 10 days (Berger, 1994). Such vast sums of money would seem ill-spent if advertising did not increase the consumption of a given product. Would the makers of Pepsi or Barbie dolls argue any differently? In 1992, Philip Morris reported profits of $4.9 billion—more than any other company in the United States. They also spent more on advertising than any other company—$2 billion (MacKenzie et al., 1994).

This leaves American society with a genuine moral, economic, and public health dilemma: Should advertising of unhealthy products be allowed when society has to pay for the diseases, disabilities, and deaths that these products cause? Tobacco companies and beer manufacturers claim that they simply influence "brand choice" and do not increase overall demand for their products (Orlandi, Lieberman, & Schinke, 1989). Moreover, they claim that because it is legal to sell their products, it should be legal to advertise them as well, and any ban represents an infringement on their First Amendment rights of commercial free speech (Gostin & Brandt, 1993; Ile & Krnoll, 1990; Shiffrin, 1993). Public health advocates counter that tobacco companies and beer manufacturers engage in unfair and deceptive practices by specifically targeting young people, using attractive role models and youth-oriented messages in their ads, and making smoking and drinking seem like normative behavior (Atkin, 1993a, 1993b; Centers for Disease Control, 1994c; Kilbourne, 1990; Madden & Grube, 1994). In other words, alcohol and tobacco manufacturers are trying to get adolescents to "just say yes" to cigarettes and beer at a time when society is trying to get them to "just say no" to drugs (Kilbourne, 1991; Strasburger, 1989c). As we shall see, the available data strongly support the public health viewpoint.

THE SIGNIFICANCE AND EPIDEMIOLOGY OF ALCOHOL AND CIGARETTE USE

Despite the fact that the "Just Say No" philosophy of the 1980s completely ignored alcohol and cigarettes, they are by far the two most significant and addictive drugs that adolescents will encounter.

First, their toll on American society is enormous. Cigarette smoking is the single most preventable cause of death in the United States, resulting in more than 400,000 deaths per year (Centers for Disease Control, 1994c). Smoking-related illnesses account for nearly one in five deaths (Bartecchi, MacKenzie, & Schrier, 1994). The Centers for Disease Control (CDC) estimates that in 1993 alone smoking cost the nation $50 billion in medical care, more than half of that paying for hospitalizations (Centers for Disease Control, 1994b). The United States is also the leading exporter of cigarettes. In fact, the United States exports three times as many cigarettes than any other country (MacKenzie et al., 1994). If current smoking rates continue, 7 million people in developing countries will die annually of smoking-related diseases. And one fifth of those living in industrialized countries will die of tobacco-related disorders (Peto, Lopez, Boreham, Thun, & Heath, 1992; "Tobacco's Toll," 1992). Although alcohol is responsible for only 100,000 deaths a year (McGinnis & Foege, 1993), it is the leading killer of adolescents because half of all automobile accidents and approximately one third of all homicides and suicides among teens involve alcohol use (Strasburger & Brown, 1991).

Second, these are the two drugs most commonly used by teenagers (Johnston, Bachman, & O'Malley, 1994). An estimated one in three teenagers smoke, including 100,000 youngsters under age 13 (Bartecchi et al., 1994; Centers for Disease Control, 1994c). Every day, an estimated 3,000 teenagers begin smoking (American Academy of Pediatrics, 1994). Experimentation is common in grade school—daily smoking usually begins between ages 12 and 14, and the chances of a young adult beginning to smoke regularly after age 21 are only 10% (American Academy of Pediatrics, 1994; Bartecchi et al., 1994; Centers for Disease Control, 1994c). Likewise, alcohol is extremely popular with younger adolescents: Two thirds of 8th graders and nearly 90% of high school seniors have tried it (Johnston et al., 1994). Even more worrisome is the fact that 14% of 8th graders and 28% of 12th graders admitted that they consumed five or more drinks in a row at least once in the 2 weeks prior to being surveyed (Johnston et al., 1994).

Third, cigarettes and alcohol represent the two most significant "gateway" drugs for teenagers. Numerous studies document that adolescent smokers and drinkers are 10 to 60 times more likely to proceed to use marijuana, cocaine, or heroin (Bailey, 1992; Centers for Disease Control, 1994c; Schonberg, 1988). Cigarettes represent the single most important gateway drug and may lead to alcohol use as well (Myers & Brown, 1994). In one study, pack-a-day smokers were 3 times more likely to use alcohol and 10 to 30 times more likely to use an illicit drug than nonsmokers (Torabi, Bailey, & Majd-Jabbari, 1993).

Fourth, these two drugs represent hugely profitable industries that require the constant recruitment of new users. Clearly, with the deaths of 1,200 smokers a day and thousands more trying to quit, the tobacco industry must recruit new smokers to remain profitable. Inevitably, these new smokers must come from the ranks of children and adolescents. In addition, selling cigarettes to children is a profitable activity itself, yielding approximately 3% of the industry's profits ($221 million in 1988) from an activity that is illegal in 43 states (DiFranza & Tye, 1990). After substantial declines in the 1970s, the prevalence of smoking among American adolescents has been stable since 1981 (Centers for Disease Control, 1992b). In the 9 years from 1981 to 1990, the rate of smoking among high school seniors fell by only 1.2%, whereas the rate among adults fell by 26%—while $24 billion was being spent promoting cigarettes (Centers for Disease Control, 1990; DiFranza, Richards, Paulman, Fletcher, & Jaffe, 1992). The alcohol industry has targeted minority groups and the young for years, particularly through the promotion of sports- and youth-oriented programming (Gerbner, 1990). Because 5% of drinkers consume 50% of all alcoholic beverages (Gerbner, 1990), new recruits are a must for the alcohol industry as well.

ADVERTISING: AN OVERVIEW

Television is a commercial medium. Indeed, many observers have commented that the "tail is now wagging the dog"—that is, programming exists solely to deliver an audience of proper demographic specifications to commercial advertisers. The larger the audience for a show, the higher the fee that can be charged per unit of commercial time. For example, during the 1994 Super Bowl, a minute of air time cost nearly $1 million.

Children in the United States view an average of 20,000 commercials per year, or a total of 360,000 by the time they graduate from high school (Strasburger, 1989b). Young children under age 8 are particularly vulnerable to television advertising because they cannot understand the nature of advertising. They believe that advertisers always tell the truth. Very young children cannot even distinguish between regular programming and commercial programming (Liebert & Sprafkin, 1988; Young, 1990). As children grow older, they gradually acquire an understanding of advertising, but the stakes increase as well. After all, young people represent a lucrative market for advertisers: Children ages 6 to 14 spend $7.3 billion a year and influence family buying of more than $120 billion a year (MacVean, 1993). Celebrity endorsers are commonly used, and older children and teenagers may be particularly vulnerable to such ads (Atkin & Block, 1983). Few commercials in the 1990s fail to employ some combination of rock music, young attractive models, humor, or adventure. Production values are extraordinary: Costs for a single 30-second commercial may easily exceed those for an entire half hour of regular programming.

A variety of studies have explored the impact of advertising on children and adolescents. Nearly all have shown advertising to be extremely effective in increasing youngsters' awareness of and emotional responses to products, their recognition of certain brands, their desire to own or use the products advertised, and their recognition of the advertisements themselves. In 1975, the National Science Foundation (1977) commissioned a report on the effects of advertising on children, which concluded:

It is clear from the available evidence that television *does* influence children. Research has demonstrated that children attend to and learn from commercials, and that advertising is at least moderately successful in creating positive attitudes toward and the desire for products advertised. (p. 179)

Although the research is not dramatically conclusive, a preponderance of *indirect* evidence points to cigarette and alcohol advertising as being a significant factor in adolescents' use of these two drugs. For alcohol, advertising may account for as much as 10% to 30% of adolescents' usage (Atkin, 1993a, 1994; Gerbner, 1990). Nevertheless, as one set of authors note:

> To reduce the argument regarding the demonstrable effects of massive advertising campaigns to the level of individual behavior is absurdly simplistic. . . . Rather, what we are dealing with is the nature of advertising itself. Pepsi Cola, for example, could not convincingly prove, through any sort of defensible scientific study, that particular children or adolescents who consume their products do so because of exposure to any or all of their ads. (Orlandi et al., 1989, p. 90)

IS COUNTER-ADVERTISING EFFECTIVE?

To be truly effective, counter-advertising must approach both the occurrence rate and the attractiveness of regular advertising (Grube & Wallack, 1994). In addition, campaigns must be intensive, well planned, and well coordinated and use media such as radio rather than rely on television or the print media alone (Bauman, LaPrelle, Brown, Koch, & Padgett, 1991; Pierce, Macaskill, & Hill, 1990). Some researchers speculate that the decrease in adolescent smoking in the mid- to late 1970s may be attributable to a very aggressive preban counter-advertising campaign in which one PSA aired for every three to five cigarette ads (Atkin, 1993b; Brown & Walsh-Childers, 1994; Madden & Grube, 1994; Wallack, Dorfman, Jernigan, & Themba, 1993). Unfortunately, part of the deal the tobacco companies made in accepting a ban on smoking ads was that antismoking ads would be eliminated as well (Gerbner, 1990). Currently, the density of public service announcements about alcohol has never remotely approached that of regular advertisements; nor are the production values comparable. Of the 685 total alcohol ads examined in one recent content analysis, only 3 contained messages about moderation and another 10 involved very brief public service announcements (e.g., "Know when to say when") (Madden & Grube, 1994).

The best-known and most sophisticated example of aggressive counter-advertising is the campaign mounted by the Partnership for a Drug-Free

TABLE 4.2 Changes in Adolescents' Attitudes About Drugs in 1987 and 1991[a]

	1987	1991
Teens who believe there is a moderate or great risk in occasional use of marijuana	63	71
Teens who believe there is a moderate or great risk in using cocaine once or twice	62	69
"Taking drugs scares me"		
Strongly agree	45	52
Somewhat agree	21	22
"People on drugs act stupidly and foolishly"		
Strongly agree	39	48
Somewhat agree	25	21

SOURCE: Data from Partnership for a Drug-Free America (1992). Adapted with permission.
[a] Values are represented in percentages.

America. Since 1987, $1.1 billion has been donated to create and air 375 antidrug public service announcements (Partnership for a Drug-Free America, 1992). The Partnership campaign has helped to turn the tide of public (and, to a lesser extent, adolescent) opinion against drugs such as marijuana and cocaine. In a recent study of nearly 1,000 public school students ages 11 to 19, more than 80% recalled exposure to such ads and half of the students who had tried drugs reported that the ads convinced them to decrease or stop using them (Reis, Duggan, Adger, & DeAngelis, 1992). Unfortunately, to date, not a single ad has aired dealing with either tobacco or alcohol. This omission is disturbing because these two drugs are by far the most significant in the United States and cause *far* more harm than marijuana or cocaine (Strasburger, 1993b). The reason should be apparent— cocaine and marijuana are easy targets; tobacco and alcohol are not because major business interests are involved. Were the Partnership to take on the task of aggressively campaigning against adolescents' use of tobacco and alcohol, the results could be impressive. However, at the moment, children and teenagers view 25 to 50 beer and wine commercials for every Partnership for a Drug-Free America ad they see (Strasburger, 1989c).

THE HISTORY OF
CIGARETTE ADVERTISING

Since 1938, the tobacco industry has engaged in a systematic campaign of public misinformation (Broder, 1992; Gerbner, 1990). It has responded

TABLE 4.3 Does Cigarette Advertising Influence Editorial Content?

Magazines	Number of Magazine-Years	Probability of Coverage of Health Care Risks (%)
All magazines		
No cigarette ads	403	11.9
Any cigarette ads	900	8.3
Women's magazines		
No cigarette ads	104	11.7
Any cigarette ads	212	5.0

SOURCE: Adapted from Warner et al., **N Engl J Med**, 1992; 326:307. © Copyright 1992. *Massachusetts Medical Society*. All rights reserved.

to increasingly conclusive scientific information by advancing its own contrary health claims, introducing king-sized and filter-tipped brands, increasing advertising budgets, targeting certain subgroups, and most recently by increasing exports to third-world countries (Barry, 1991; Wallack & Montgomery, 1992). In 1964, following the Surgeon General's report on smoking and health, the Federal Trade Commission decided that cigarette advertising that failed to disclose the health risks of smoking was "unfair and deceptive" (Liebert & Sprafkin, 1988). In the late 1960s, public health activists used the FCC's "fairness doctrine" to force broadcasters to air antismoking public service announcements. As cigarette sales began falling, the tobacco industry volunteered to discontinue broadcast advertisements, and Congress accepted the offer by passing the Public Health Cigarette Smoking Act of 1969 that banned all such ads beginning in 1971.

However, the congressional ban hardly put an end to cigarette advertising. It merely drove the ads into more newspapers, magazines, and billboards (Centers for Disease Control, 1990). Moreover, this situation resulted in a "chilling effect" on the editorial content of many magazines. Several studies in the 1980s and 1990s have documented that as the amount of cigarette advertising in a magazine increases, the amount of coverage of health risks associated with smoking decreases dramatically (Amos, Jacobson, & White, 1991; DeJong, 1995; Kessler, 1989; Signorielli, 1990; Smith, 1978; Warner, 1985; Warner, Goldenhar, & McLaughlin, 1992; Weis & Burke, 1986; Whelan, Sheridan, Meister, & Mosher, 1981). Most recently, researchers using a logistic-regression analysis to examine 99 American magazines published over a 25-year span (between 1959-1969 and 1973-1986) found that the probability of publishing an article on the risks of smoking decreased 38% for magazines that derived significant revenue from tobacco companies (Warner et al., 1992). Women's magazines are particularly guilty. A study of *Cosmopolitan, Good Housekeeping, Mademoiselle, McCall's,* and *Women's Day* found that between 1983 and 1987, not one of them published a single column or feature on the dangers of smoking (Kessler, 1989). All but *Good Housekeeping* accept cigarette advertising. This occurred exactly during the same 5-year period that lung cancer was surpassing breast cancer as the number one killer of women (Moog, 1991).

IMPACT OF CIGARETTE ADVERTISING ON TEENAGERS

Cigarette advertising appears to increase teenagers' risk of smoking by affecting their image of smokers and smoking (Centers for Disease Control, 1994c). Smoking is glamorized. Smokers are depicted as independent, healthy, youthful, and adventurous. Adverse consequences or noxious side effects of smoking are never shown. Interestingly, nearly half of eighth graders do not believe that smoking a pack of cigarettes a day represents a health risk (Johnston et al., 1994). Numerous studies show that children who pay closer attention to cigarette advertisements or who can recall such ads more readily are more likely to view smoking favorably and become smokers themselves (Aitken & Eadie, 1990; Armstrong, de Klerk, Shean, Dunn, & Dolin, 1990; Centers for Disease Control, 1992a; Goldstein, Fischer, Richards, & Creten, 1987; Klitzner, Gruenewald, & Bamberger, 1991; Vickers, 1992). In teenage girls, smoking rates increased dramatically around 1967, exactly the same time when women were being targeted by such new brands as Virginia Slims (Pierce, Lee, & Gilpin, 1994). Only a rare study can be found that shows tobacco advertising has *no* influence on children (Smith, 1989).

Of course, peer pressure is important during adolescence as well, as is parental example, but these must be placed in a proper perspective:

> Teens and preteens somehow get the idea that smoking makes one sexy, athletic, cool, or macho. The tobacco industry says these ideas come from their peers. No one asks where these peers—other kids—get these ideas. Yet about the only place in our society where these silly images occur is advertising. So-called peer pressure explains little. It is merely a clever term used to shift blame from the manufacturer and advertiser to the user. Like peer pressure, "parental example" does not just spontaneously occur. Parents of today started smoking as children, and no doubt had similar silly ideas about what smoking would do for their images. (DiFranza et al., 1992, p. 3282)

In 1991, the *Journal of the American Medical Association* published a remarkable set of studies that add further credence to the notion that tobacco advertising has a significant impact on young people:

1. A study of RJR Nabisco's current Joe Camel cartoon-theme advertising found that the ads effectively target children. Joe Camel is a James Bond-type figure who rides motorcycles, shoots pool, chats up beautiful women, and smokes while looking exceptionally cool. Compared with adults, more than twice as many children who reported exposure to Joe Camel were able to recognize the association with Camel cigarettes and found such ads appealing (DiFranza et al., 1991). Not coincidentally, in the 3 years after the introduction of the Joe Camel campaign, the preference for Camels increased from 0.5% of adolescent smokers to 32%. During the same time period, the sale of Camels to minors increased from $6 million to $476 million, representing one quarter of all Camel sales and one third of all illegal cigarette sales to minors (DiFranza et al., 1991).

2. A separate study found that 6-year-olds are as likely to recognize Joe Camel as the famous mouseketeer logo for the Disney Channel (Fischer, Schwart, Richards, Goldstein, & Rojas, 1991). Even at age 3, 30% of children could still make the association between the Joe Camel figure and a pack of cigarettes.

3. A California study documented that the most heavily advertised brands of cigarettes—Marlboro and Camel—were the most popular among teenage smokers (Pierce et al., 1991). A similar national study by the CDC found that 84% of teenagers purchased Marlboros, Camels, or Newports—the three most highly advertised brands in the United States in 1990 (Centers for Disease Control, 1992b). Their ad campaigns are represented by the Marlboro Man, Joe Camel, and fun-loving couples, respectively. Yet these three brands capture only 35% of *overall* sales. In England, the most popular brands of cigarettes among teenagers (Benson & Hedges, Silk Cut, Embassy, and Marlboro) are likewise the most heavily advertised (Vickers, 1992).

An ongoing case in Canada challenging the constitutionality of the Tobacco Products Control Act of 1988 has revealed internal tobacco company documents that describe how the industry specifically targets young people and, in fact, believes that advertising *does* influence them to become smokers (Mintz, 1991). A naturalistic experiment is also relevant: At the same time that televised cigarette advertising has been banned,

JOE CAMEL —
THE LATER
YEARS

HACK!
HACK!!
HACK!!

smokeless tobacco products have not. Until 1986, both print and broadcast media were rife with such advertising. Smokeless tobacco companies also sponsored tobacco-spitting contests and marketing programs in colleges. Not surprisingly, the prevalence of smokeless tobacco use among teenagers has increased dramatically (DiFranza et al., 1992; Gottlieb, Pope, Rickert, & Hardin, 1993).

The weight of the evidence is such that the U.S. Surgeon General recently concluded:

> Cigarette advertising appears to affect young people's perceptions of the pervasiveness, image, and function of smoking. Since misperceptions in these areas constitute psychosocial risk factors for the initiation of smoking, *cigarette advertising appears to increase young people's risk of smoking.* (Centers for Disease Control, 1994c, p. 195; emphasis added)

Several research studies also give insights into some of the suggested remedies. For example, teenagers spend only 8% of their viewing time reading warning labels in print ads, compared with 92% of their time viewing the advertisements themselves (Fischer, Richards, Berman, & Krugman, 1989). Rather than serve as a caution to teenagers, warning labels may be accomplishing nothing more than immunizing tobacco manufacturers against product liability suits (Brown & Walsh-Childers, 1994). On the other hand, advertising bans do seem to be effective (Pollay, 1991). In New Zealand, consumption fell after a complete ban on cigarette advertising (Vickers, 1992). In Norway, the prevalence of 13- to 15-year-old smokers decreased from 17% in 1975 to 10% in 1990 after an advertising ban was imposed (Vickers, 1992). A recent analysis of factors influencing tobacco consumption in 22 countries revealed that since 1973 advertising restrictions have resulted in lower rates of smoking (Laugesen & Meads, 1991).

CIGARETTES IN TELEVISION PROGRAMMING AND MOVIES

The portrayal of smokers on television shows that the entertainment industry *can* be sensitive to public health issues. Between 1950 and 1982, smoking steadily decreased on television (Breed & De Foe, 1984). Before the Surgeon General's landmark 1964 report on smoking, TV characters smoked nine times more frequently than in 1982 (Signorielli, 1990). Only 2% of series stars smoke on TV (Breed & De Foe, 1983). However, TV programs also rarely show characters refusing to smoke or expressing anti-

TABLE 4.4 Seven Myths Alcohol Advertisers Want Adolescents to Believe

1. *Everyone* drinks alcohol.
2. Drinking has no risks.
3. Drinking helps to solve problems.
4. Alcohol is a magic potion that can transform you.
5. Sports and alcohol go together.
6. If alcohol were truly dangerous, we wouldn't be advertising it.
7. Alcoholic beverage companies only promote drinking in moderation.

SOURCE: Kilbourne (1991). Adapted with permission from author and *Media & Values.*

smoking sentiments—probably so as not to offend the corporate advertisers whose parent companies also own tobacco subsidiaries (Signorielli,
1990).

Unfortunately, in the movies, smoking seems to be making a dramatic
comeback. A recent study found that since 1960, the top-grossing films
have shown movie stars lighting up at three times the rate of American adults
(Hazan, Lipton, & Glantz, 1994). Unlike in real life, smoking rates in the
movies have not changed between 1960 and 1990. Movie smokers tend
to be white, middle-class male characters who are usually the heroes (Hazan
et al., 1994). Use of passive advertising—so-called "product place-
ments"—is also a problem on the big screen. The Philip Morris Company
reportedly paid $350,000 to place Lark cigarettes in the James Bond
movie *License to Kill* and another $42,500 to place Marlboros in *Super-
man II* ("Selling to Children," 1990).

ALCOHOL ADVERTISING

Like cigarette ads in the print media, beer commercials are virtually
custom-made to appeal to children and adolescents: images of fun-loving,
sexy, successful young people having the time of their lives. Who wouldn't
want to indulge? But unlike cigarette advertising, beer and wine ads flood
the airwaves: Children and teenagers view 1,000 to 2,000 of them annually
(Strasburger, 1989c). Rarely do they see ads or public service announcements urging moderation (Madden & Grube, 1994). Perhaps as a result,
nearly three fourths of American adults think that such advertising encourages teenagers to drink (Lipman, 1991).

Content analyses show that beer ads seem to suggest that drinking is an
absolutely harmless activity with no major health risks associated with it
(Atkin, 1993a; Atkin, DeJong, & Wallack, 1992; Atkin, Hocking, & Block,

1984; Grube, 1993; Grube & Wallack, 1994; Madden & Grube, 1994; Postman, Nystrom, Strate, & Weingartner, 1988; Strasburger, 1993b; Wallack, Cassady, & Grube, 1990). Yet more than one third of ads show people driving or engaging in water sports while supposedly drinking (Madden & Grube, 1994). In the most recent study, Madden and Grube (1994) examined a random sample of more than 150 sports events and nearly 450 hours of network programming from 1990 to 1992. Major sports programming contained 2.4 ads per hour, with another 3.3 ads per hour coming from passive ads.

IMPACT OF ALCOHOL
ADVERTISING ON ADOLESCENTS

Adolescents comprehend alcohol advertising quite well by age 14 (Aitken, Eadie, Leathar, McNeill, & Scott, 1988; Grube, 1993). By age 16, they list beer ads among their favorites (Wallack et al., 1990). But even children under 16 may be vulnerable. In a recent survey of fifth and sixth graders, for example, nearly 60% could identify Spuds McKenzie and more than 80% could match him with Budweiser beer (Wallack et al., 1990).

Surprisingly little research has been done on the effect of advertising on adolescents' actual drinking behavior. Instead, most studies have dealt with the effect of advertising on adolescents' attitudes or their intentions to drink. Evidence does exist that the alcohol industry, like its first cousin the tobacco industry, targets young people and that underage drinkers *are* more heavily influenced by such advertising (Aitken et al., 1988; Barton, 1989; Buchanan & Lev, 1990; Grube, 1993; Lieberman & Orlandi, 1987; Postman et al., 1988; Singer, 1985a; Wallack et al., 1990). For example, in a unique, ongoing longitudinal study, Grube and Wallack (1994) have found that fifth and sixth graders who are more aware of alcohol advertising have more positive beliefs about drinking and can recognize more brands and slogans.

In addition, experimental data from four different studies demonstrate that using sexual imagery (Atkin, 1994; Kilbourne, Painton, & Ridley, 1985) or celebrity endorsers (Atkin & Block, 1983; Friedman, Termini, & Washington, 1977) increases the impact of beer and wine ads on young people. In one laboratory study of fifth and sixth graders, boys who saw programming that showed the main characters using alcohol were more likely to think positively about alcohol (Kotch, Coulter, & Lipsitz, 1986).

There is also a small but demonstrable effect of exposure to beer and wine commercials on actual drinking behavior among teenagers (Atkin et al., 1984; Bailey, 1992) and college students (Kohn & Smart, 1984, 1987). A few correlational surveys have been done. In two, a moderate positive association exists between exposure to beer and wine advertisements and excessive consumption or drinking while driving (Atkin, Neuendorf, & McDermott, 1983). Another study showed that heavy viewers were more likely to drink alcohol than light or moderate viewers (Tucker, 1985): Presumably the exposure to advertising is greater. Other research also suggests:

- Since 1960 in the United States, a dramatic increase in advertising expenditures has been accompanied by a 50% per capita increase in alcohol consumption (Jacobson & Collins, 1985).
- In Sweden, a mid-1970s ban on all beer and wine advertising resulted in a 20% per capita drop in alcohol consumption (Romelsjo, 1987).
- Like cigarette warning labels, alcohol warning labels are probably ineffective (MacKinnon, Pentz, & Stacy, 1993).
- In one study of suburban Maryland 8- to 12-year-olds, the children were able to name more brand names of beer than U.S. presidents (Center for Science in the Public Interest, 1988).
- A 1990 study of 468 randomly selected fifth and sixth graders found that 88% of them could identify Spuds Mackenzie with Bud Light beer. Their ability to name brands of beer and match slogans with the brands was significantly related to their exposure and attention to beer ads. The greater the exposure and attention, the greater the likelihood that the children would think that drinking is associated with fun and good times, not health risks, and that the children expected to drink as adults. Their attitudes about drinking were especially conditioned by watching weekend sports programming on TV (Wallack et al., 1990).

Clearly, advertising *is* effective—particularly with young, impressionable viewers. Although there is always the possibility that adolescent drinkers search out or attend to alcohol advertising more than their abstinent peers, this seems considerably less likely (Atkin, 1990; Grube, 1993). One advertising executive has noted that if extensive advertising doesn't produce bigger profits, then something is wrong with the people who make the budgets (Samuelson, 1991).

ALCOHOL IN TELEVISION
PROGRAMMING AND MOVIES

During the 1970s and early 1980s, alcohol was ubiquitous on American television—the most popular beverage consumed—and negative consequences of drinking were rarely shown or discussed (Breed & De Foe,

1981, 1984). Especially on soap operas, alcohol was depicted as an excellent social lubricant and an easy means of resolving serious personal crises (Lowery, 1980). When the public health community voiced its concern, Hollywood responded with new guidelines for the industry, issued by the Caucus of Producers, Writers, and Directors, designed to avoid (1) gratuitously using alcohol in programming, (2) glamorizing drinking, (3) showing it as a macho activity, or (4) depicting drinking with no serious consequences (Breed & De Foe, 1982; Caucus for Producers, Writers, and Directors, 1983). Recently, the Harvard School of Public Health initiated the Harvard Alcohol Project in collaboration with major networks and studios to develop programming specifically aimed at attacking the problem of drunken driving (Rothenberg, 1988).

But a 1986 content analysis suggested that alcohol is still extremely common on TV and in the movies: 100% of theatrical or made-for-TV movies and more than 75% of all dramatic series contained some mention of it (Wallack, Grube, Madden, & Breed, 1990). Of the 16 most popular R-rated movies in the mid-1980s seen frequently by teenagers in Greenberg et al.'s study (1993), every film contained alcohol use, with an average of 16 episodes per film.

Much of the alcohol use portrayed in both media is unnecessary to the plot, and drinking is still being presented as problem free. Although underage drinking on TV is rare (less than 2% of all portrayals), adolescent drinking is often treated in a humorous fashion and teens frequently acknowledge a desire to drink as a symbol of adulthood (De Foe & Breed, 1988).

Only one content analysis has been done thus far in the 1990s. Compared with earlier analyses, drinking episodes remain frequent: 6 per hour in 1991 versus 10 per hour in 1984 and 5 per hour in 1976 (Grube, 1993; Wallack et al., 1990). Primetime drinkers are usually familiar, high-status characters. More than 50% of the programs examined had a character drinking, and more than 80% contained references to alcohol (Grube, 1993).

A few TV shows have taken the lead and have dealt with alcohol use and alcoholism in a responsible manner: *Cagney & Lacey, Murphy Brown, Sisters,* and, in particular, *Beverly Hills 90210* and *Blossom*—shows extremely popular with teenagers and preteenagers. In addition, in the 1993 to 1995 seasons, more characters seem to be choosing nonalcoholic beverages than ever before. The days of having a character pour a drink as a means of making a transition from one scene to the next seem to be over. But, clearly, any changes toward healthier programming are far outweighed by the sheer volume of alcohol ads with their deceptive and unhealthy messages.

CONCLUSION: *RES IPSA LOQUITUR*

In law, there is an important principle called *Res Ipsa Loquitur*—"the thing speaks for itself." In certain tort cases, there is no way of proving negligence conclusively: A plane crashes, everyone in it is killed, and there are no eyewitnesses. Could the pilot have been responsible because he operated the aircraft in a negligent fashion? A circumstantial case must be constructed. On the basis of this evidence, a judge or jury can conclude that a defendant was negligent, even though no direct eyewitness evidence supports that he was. So, too, with cigarette and alcohol advertising and its impact on children and adolescents. Studies show that young people attend to cigarette and alcohol ads, are influenced by them, and that consumption decreases in the absence of such ads. Additional evidence exists that tobacco and beer companies actually target young people with particular advertising. Thus the preponderance of evidence suggests that the tobacco and alcohol industries profit illegally and irresponsibly from marketing their products to children and teenagers. In the final chapter, specific solutions to this current situation will be examined in the context of improving all aspects of the media for children and adolescents.

In a decade when "just say no" have become watchwords for many parents and school programs, unprecedented amounts of money are being spent in an effort to induce teenagers to "just say yes" to smoking and drinking, with virtually no concern about what age they begin either activity. Half of all the tobacco industry's profits come from sales of cigarettes to people who first became addicted to nicotine as children and adolescents (DiFranza & Tye, 1990). As one group of researchers suggests, the "discussion [should] be *elevated* from the scientific and legal arenas to the domain of ethics and social responsibility" (Orlandi et al., 1989, p. 92, my italics). Clearly, advertising and programming create a demand for cigarettes and alcohol among children and teenagers. Ironically, the situation seems analogous to one depicted in a *New Yorker* cartoon: The Frobush Purification factory is situated on a river downstream from the Frobush Industrial Pollution factory. As he gazes out the window, the president of the two companies tells the Board of Directors that they create the mess *and* they clean it up. As a result, business has never been better. Likewise, the comments of one public health activist about smoking apply equally to drinking:

In a real sense, the issue is not about advertising, but whether this industry is acting in a socially responsible manner, especially where the future health and well-being of our children are concerned. If we are to take seriously the stated industry position that they do not want children to smoke, they would take the only responsible course of action available and immediately cease all such youth-oriented promotions. (Broder, 1992, p. 783)

5

NUTRITION

Television presents viewers with two sets of conflicting messages. One suggests that we eat in ways almost guaranteed to make us fat; the other suggests that we strive to remain slim.

Kaufman, 1980, p. 45

Although sex, drugs, rock 'n' roll, and violence grab the headlines and represent major health concerns during adolescence, the media have an important impact on other areas of adolescent health as well. Television nutrition—in particular, the impact of food advertising—is coming under increasing scrutiny.

OVERVIEW

Food Advertisements. American children view an estimated 20,000 advertisements per year (Strasburger, 1992). More than half of such ads are for food (Brown & Walsh-Childers, 1994), especially sugared cereals and high-caloric snacks (Center for Science in the Public Interest, 1992; Jeffrey, McLellarn, & Fox, 1982). Healthy foods are advertised less than 3% of the time (Kunkel & Gantz, 1991). Research clearly indicates that such ads effectively get younger children to request more junk food and attempt to influence their parents' purchases (Liebert & Sprafkin, 1988).

Food in Television Programming. Food references occur nearly 10 times per hour on primetime TV, and 60% are for low-nutrient snacks or beverages (Story & Faulkner, 1990). Snacking occurs as frequently as break-fast, lunch, and dinner combined (Gerbner et al., 1980a). On Saturday morning TV, 61% of commercials are for food and more than 90% of those are for sugared cereals, candy bars, fast foods, chips, or other nutritionally unsound foods (Center for Science in the Public Interest, 1992).

75

Obesity. National surveys document that the prevalence of obesity is increasing in the United States. Currently, one in three adults is 20% or more above their desirable weight for height (Kuczmarski, Flegal, Campbell, & Johnson, 1994). Studies also show that obese young women have lower incomes, are less likely to marry, and have completed less schooling (Gortmaker, Must, Perrin, Sobol, & Dietz, 1993). By age 7, children have already learned norms of cultural attractiveness and are more likely to choose a playmate with a major physical handicap than one who is obese (Feldman, Feldman, & Goodman, 1988; Staffieri, 1967). An adolescent's self-concept is usually sufficiently tenuous that any physical characteristic causing him or her to be different represents a potential threat to self-esteem (Willis, McCoy, & Berman, 1990). By third grade, nearly one third of boys and girls have already tried to lose weight (Maloney, McGuire, Daniels, & Specker, 1989).

Along with aggression, obesity represents one of the two areas of television research in which the medium's influence achieves the level of cause-and-effect rather than simply being contributory (American Academy of Pediatrics, 1990). Using National Health Survey data, Dietz found that hours spent watching TV proved to be a strong predictor of adolescent obesity, with the prevalence increasing 2% for each additional hour of average television viewing above the norm (Dietz & Gortmaker, 1985). A recent attempt to duplicate these findings failed (Robinson et al., 1993) but involved a smaller sample and did not use national data (Dietz & Gortmaker, 1993). Other recent studies have found that numbers of hours of TV watched is a strong predictor for high cholesterol levels in children (Wong et al., 1992) and that children who watch a lot of TV are more likely to have poor eating habits and unhealthy notions about food (Signorielli & Lears, 1992).

Why might this association exist? The excess intake of only 50 kcals per day can account for a weight gain of 5 pounds per year (Dietz, 1993). Therefore, even if television viewing exerts only a slight effect, it may be highly significant. Because obesity is caused by an imbalance of excess intake compared with energy expenditure, TV viewing may contribute in several ways:

1. *Displacement of more active pursuits.* As the leading leisure-time activity, television constitutes the principal source of *in*activity for children and adolescents (Dietz, 1993). Williams' naturalistic study (1986) found that children participated less in sports activities once TV was introduced into their community. In the United States, data from the

National Children and Youth Fitness Survey show that parents' and teachers' ratings of a child's activity level and time spent watching TV correlated directly with their prevalence of obesity (Dietz, 1993). Clearly, if children and adolescents devoted just 1 hour a day to physical activities of the 3 hours they spend watching TV, their risk of obesity would diminish considerably.

2. *Increased energy intake.* Television deluges young viewers with advertisements for food products and fast food restaurants that provide marginal nutritional value at best. In addition, primetime and Saturday morning programming models poor nutritional behavior for children. Time spent watching TV correlates with children's attempts to influence their parents' food purchases, children's choice of snacks, the frequency they snack while watching TV, and their total caloric intake (Dietz, 1993; Taras, Sallis, Patterson, Nader, & Nelson, 1989). In a recent study of 209 fourth- and fifth-grade students, Signorielli and Lears (1992) found that heavy TV viewing was an extremely strong predictor of poor nutritional habits and that heavy viewers were far more likely to believe that fast food was as nutritious as a meal prepared at home. Although no studies have specifically examined adolescents' television viewing and their food-buying habits, one study has found that both children and adolescents tend to consume higher-fat food products if they watch a lot of television (Wong et al., 1992).

3. *Decreased energy expenditure.* One recent study has found that television viewing may significantly lower one's metabolic rate (Klesges, Shelton, & Klesges, 1993), although the results have not yet been replicated (Dietz, 1993). But several studies do indicate that television viewing may adversely affect physical fitness (Dietz, 1993; Robinson et al., 1993; Tucker, 1985).

Eating Disorders. With the incidence of anorexia nervosa as high as 1 in 100 to 150 middle-class females (Strasburger & Brown, 1991), and the incidence of bulimia as high as 10% (Killen et al., 1986), some researchers have looked accusingly at media portrayals of food. For example, studies show that TV primetime characters are usually happy in the presence of food, but food is rarely used to satisfy hunger. Rather it serves to bribe others or to facilitate social introductions (Kaufman, 1980). As with other media, television seems to have an obsession with thinness: 88% of all characters are thin or average in body build, obesity is confined to middle or old age, and being overweight provides comic ammunition (Kaufman, 1980).

As previously mentioned, body image is a major concern of teenagers, especially females. A recent survey of 326 adolescent females attending an upper-middle-class parochial high school found that the students demonstrated exaggerated fears of obesity regardless of their actual body weight. More than half of the underweight students described themselves as being extremely fearful of becoming obese, and more than one third were preoccupied with their body fat (Moses, Banilivy, & Lifshitz, 1989). Unfortunately, the media (and society) seem to have a very distorted view of the "ideal" woman. In a study of body measurements of Playboy center-folds and Miss America contestants over a 10-year period, researchers found that body weight averaged 13% to 19% below that expected for their ages. At the same time, there was a significant increase in articles about dieting and exercise in six women's magazines. The authors concluded that there is an "overvaluation of thinness" (Wiseman, Gray, Mosimann, & Ahrens, 1992).

Aside from the portrayal of "Roseanne" as being overweight, hip, and in control, one other attempt to reverse this trend has been the British Broadcasting Corporation's 1985 ban on televising beauty pageants, la-belling them "an anachronism in this day and age of equality and verging on the offensive" ("BBC Bans Beauty Contest," 1985).

CONCLUSION

Considerable data exist to justify the notion that the media make a significant impact on adolescents' eating habits and the occurrence of obesity during childhood and adolescence, and perhaps even contribute in a small way to the development of eating disorders.

6

ROCK MUSIC AND MUSIC VIDEOS

Sex sells in America, and as the advertising world has grown ever more risque in pushing cars, cosmetics, jeans, and liquor to adults, pop music has been forced further past the fringes of respectability for its rebellious thrills. When Mom and Dad watch a Brut commercial in which a nude woman puts on her husband's shirt and sensuously rubs his after-shave all over herself, well, what can a young boy do? Play in a rock 'n' roll band and be a bit more outrageous than his parents want him to be. Kids' natural anti-authoritarianism is going to drive them to the frontiers of sexual fantasy in a society where most aspects of the dirty deed have been appropriated by racy advertising and titillating TV cheesecakery.

Terence Moran,
The New Republic, 1985, p. 15. Reprinted with permission.

ROCK 'N' ROLL MUSIC

When Little Richard sang "Good Golly, Miss Molly" in 1959, he was not singing about a young woman with hay fever and middle ear problems. Nor was the Rolling Stones's 1960s hit "Let's Spend the Night Together" about a vacationing family planning to stay at a Motel-6. In fact, the producers of *The Ed Sullivan Show* insisted that the Rolling Stones change the lyrics to "Let's spend some time together" before they could even appear on the show. And perhaps the most famous ambiguous rock song ever recorded—"Louie, Louie" by the Kingsmen—was played speeded up, slowed down, and backwards before the FCC decided in 1962 that it was unintelligible at any speed (Marsh, 1993; Moran, 1985). Rock lyrics and rock music have always been controversial and problematic to adult society.

TABLE 6.1 Teenagers' Tastes in Modern Music[a] ($N = 2,760$ 14- to 16-year-olds; 68% white; 32% black)

Favorite Type of Music		Groups Most Often Named	
Rock	31	Bon Jovi	10
		U2	2
Rap	18	Run DMC	6
		LL Cool J	4
		Beastie Boys	4
Soul	18	New Edition	3
Heavy metal	13	Motley Crue	2
		Poison	2

SOURCE: Adapted from Klein et al. (1993). Reproduced by permission of *Pediatrics*.
[a] Values are represented in percentages.

Of course, suggestive song lyrics did not originate with 1950s rock 'n' roll. From Cole Porter ("The Lady Is a Tramp"; "Let's Do It") to classic blues songs like "Hootchie Cootchie Man," American songwriters and singers in the 20th century have seemed obsessed with seeing how much they can get away with. Yet there is no question that lyrics *have* gotten more provocative and explicit in the past 2 decades (Fedler, Hall, & Tanzi, 1982; Hendren & Strasburger, 1993). On the other hand, rock 'n' roll *must* be provocative, antiestablishment, and disliked by adults to a certain extent. Rock music is an important badge of identity for adolescents and an important activity for them.

Rock music has unique effects on adolescents because it is an aural medium and one in which exposure does not typically begin until early adolescence. Presumably, teenagers will have developed greater critical faculties and be less resistant to media influences at age 14 than at age 4. That is not necessarily the case with music videos, which are visual (and therefore as potent as television) and are popular with preteenagers as well.

Definition of Terms. The terms *rock music* and *popular music* will be used interchangeably to indicate music currently listened to by teenagers. The terms include hard rock, soft rock, punk rock, heavy metal, rap, grunge, salsa, and soul music. Different genres of music are popular with different racial and ethnic groups, although there is considerable crossover. Teenagers' choice in music helps them to define important social and subcultural boundaries (Christenson & Roberts, 1990).

Heavy metal and rap music have elicited the greatest concern. Once considered as only a fringe category of rock music, heavy metal is characterized by the loud, pulsating rhythms of electric bass guitar and drums and the seeming obsession with themes of violence, dominance and abuse of women, hate, the occult, satanism, and death (Arnett, 1991). Groups such as Metallica, Black Sabbath, Megadeath, Slayer, and AC/DC have gained increasing notoriety. In 1989, the group Guns-N-Roses reported a 2-year income of more than $20 million ("Entertainers Have the Last Laugh," 1990). One reason for the apparent upswing in popularity of heavy metal music is that mainstream rock 'n' roll music has already been co-opted by much of adult society. Some parents and parent groups have advocated censorship, but clearly that is not an acceptable or legal solution (American Academy of Pediatrics, 1989; Hendren & Strasburger, 1993). In October 1992 the U.S. Supreme Court let stand lower court rulings declaring that heavy metal rock star Ozzy Osbourne's free speech rights protected him against lawsuits brought by the parents of two teenagers in Georgia and South Carolina who had committed suicide after listening to his song "Suicide Solution." Two other suicides were attributed to alleged subliminal messages of "do it" in Judas Priest's song "Beyond the Realms of Death" ("Families Sue Band," 1990). In all such cases, lawsuits against the recording artists have failed.

Rap music has its roots in black culture and is characterized by talking to a musical beat. At times, it is angry and violent (e.g., gangsta rap). Several rappers, including Snoop Doggy Dogg and Tupac Shakur, have had well-publicized encounters with the law (Leland, 1993). "Cop Killer," one notable song by rapper Ice-T, describes shooting and killing cops. Police organizations from around the country demanded the recall of the recording (Leland, 1992). Although Warner Brothers Records refused, Ice-T asked that the track be removed from all future productions of the album. Rap music is not unidimensional, however. At times, it can also be prosocial, embracing such traditional social values as nurturance, education, and self-sufficiency (Leland, 1992). In fact, no other music style has so many antidrug songs (Pareles, 1990).

Consumption. As television viewing begins to wane during mid- to late adolescence, listening to rock music increases. In one survey of 2,760 14- to 16-year-olds in 10 different urban Southeast centers, listening to music averaged 40 hours per week (Klein et al., 1993). In a survey of California teens, consumption was lower—2 ½ to 3 hours per day—although the total average daily time spent with broadcast media was 7 hours (Christenson & Roberts, 1990). Often, music is used as a background accompaniment to doing homework, driving, or talking with friends. There is no evidence that music media exert a displacement effect on other activities such as schoolwork (Christenson & Roberts, 1990), although several studies suggest that teens who spend more time listening to music tend to do less well academically (Burke & Grinder, 1966; Larson & Kubey, 1983) and that students who study while listening to rock music exhibit lower comprehension of the material than students studying in silence or listening to classical music (LaVoie & Collins, 1975). However, with the exception of the comprehension study, these studies do not establish cause-and-effect, only associations. Given the importance of popular music in adolescents' lives, the lack of research into its effects on academic performance seems rather surprising.

Why Adolescents Like Rock Music. The uses (and abuses) of popular music are myriad. Main categories include:

- Relaxation and mood regulation
- Social (partying, talking with friends, playing)
- Silence-filling (background noise, relief from boredom)
- Expressive (identification with a particular sound, lyrics, or musical group)

When teenagers are asked about the appeal of rock music, they respond that they are most interested in "the beat," not the lyrics. Yet even if lyric content remains unimportant to them on a conscious level, that does not exonerate provocative lyrics or dismiss the possibility that teens can learn from them. As two experts note, "We don't drive down the freeway in order to see billboards, but we see them and we acquire information from them" anyway (Christenson & Roberts, 1990, p. 28).

Music does play an important role in the socialization of adolescents. It can help them identify with a peer group (Roe, 1990) or serve as an important symbol of antiestablishment rebellion (Strasburger, 1990). The performers of popular music also have a significant role in adolescent development as potential role models. And with adolescent consumers estimated to have $73 billion worth of purchasing power, mainstream advertising is now saturated with rock 'n' roll music. In fact, as one critic asserts, rock 'n' roll has actually become the voice of corporate America (Frith, 1992). But the questions that need to be asked regarding the influence of popular music on adolescents are: Which music? Which adolescents? At what stage of development? With what coping abilities and environmental stresses?

The antiestablishment nature of rock music and its importance in adolescent identity formation is a complex issue. One view is that "young people use music to resist authority at all levels, assert their personalities, develop peer relationships and romantic entanglements, and learn about things that their parents and the schools aren't telling them" (Lull, 1987, p. 152). Another critic maintains that the critical job of music is to divide the cultural world into Us and Them (Grossberg, 1992). Only one experimental study has addressed this issue directly: a longitudinal study of Swedish youth and rock music (Roe, 1984). Early converts to rock music (age 11) were more likely to be influenced by their peers and less influenced by their parents than older adolescents. Because this was a longitudinal study, the investigator could use statistical analyses to demonstrate that it was the early age of music involvement that *caused* the increased influence of the peer group over parents.

On the other hand, most rock 'n' roll—aside from heavy metal and gangsta rap—is surprisingly mainstream in its value orientation (Christenson & Roberts, 1990). Romantic love is still the most prevalent theme, despite the fact that the lyrics have become more explicit and the treatment of love is less romantic and more physical (Fedler et al., 1982). In addition, a more modern or revisionist view of normal adolescent psychology would say that the *sturm und drang* ("storm and stress") of adolescence is inaccurate, and that most teenagers never consciously identify rock music as a way of driving a rift between themselves and their parents (Christenson & Roberts, 1990).

The following case vignettes illustrate the important role rock music can play in the life of an adolescent and how one cannot talk about the effect of such music without talking about the individual adolescent (Hendren & Strasburger, 1993):

Case 1: Sean was a 16-year-old emotionally reserved boy whose parents ended their marriage in an acrimonious divorce 3 years earlier. Because of parental fighting, Sean saw little of his father and when he did, they usually had a fight about the father's young girlfriend. Sean was extremely interested in the martial arts and heavy metal music. After school, he often went into his room and read martial arts books while listening to groups such as Metallica and Slayer. He reported feeling less alone and angry after this, although it upset his conservative mother. Sean has never been violent and continues to be emotionally reserved and socially withdrawn. Currently he is attending law school.

Case 2: Owen was a 15-year-old boy whose parents are bright university professors who were adolescents during the 60s. They became concerned that Owen might be involved with drugs because he was very interested in acid rock and the music associated with the drug culture in the 60s. Owen was bright but not doing well in school. He said he found it difficult to do as well as his successful parents. He tried recreational drugs but stopped drug use around age 17. Currently, he is attending a liberal arts university and identifies with the "artsy liberal types" there.

Case 3: Kurt was a 17-year-old boy whose parents divorced when he was young. He had limited contact with his alcoholic father. Kurt always had trouble in school and also had some minor trouble with the law. He became involved in a satanic cult in which he and others frequently listened to heavy metal rock. He was hospitalized in an adolescent psychiatric hospital after a suicide attempt. While there, he admitted to being involved in several human sacrifices as part of the satanic cult.

Adolescents' Comprehension of Song Lyrics. If there is "good" news about the increasingly explicit lyrics of popular music, it is that many teenagers do not know the lyrics or comprehend their intended meaning. For example, in one study only 30% of teenagers knew the lyrics to their favorite songs (Greenfield et al., 1987). Even if the students knew the lyrics, their comprehension varied greatly. For example, only 10% of fourth graders could correctly interpret a Madonna song, none could correctly interpret a Springsteen song, and nearly 50% of college students thought that "Born in the U.S.A." was a song of patriotism, not alienation (Greenfield et al., 1987). Other studies have found similarly low rates of lyric knowledge or comprehension (Denisoff & Levine, 1971; Leming, 1987; Prinsky & Rosenbaum, 1987).

Heavy metal music devotees seem to be the exception. In Greenfield et al.'s study (1987), 40% knew the lyrics to their favorite songs. Other studies have found that these teenagers are more likely to listen closely to the lyrics, to feel that the music represents a very important part of their lives, and to identify with the performers (Arnett, 1991; Wass et al., 1988).

Comprehension of lyrics increases with age (Hendren & Strasburger, 1993). Even so, whereas adults frequently identify such themes as sex, drugs, violence, and satanism in current rock music, teenagers tend to interpret that their favorite songs are about "love, friendship, growing up, life's struggles, having fun, cars, religion, and other topics that relate to teenage life" (Prinsky & Rosenbaum, 1987, p. 393).

Of course, these studies assess comprehension using an adult norm (Christenson & Roberts, 1990). Theoretically, the adult interpretation could be incorrect, or the incorrect interpretation could still be having significant behavioral impact. In addition, the small percentage of teens who actually do know the lyrics or comprehend their meaning might be precisely those who are at the highest risk. Alternatively, those who comprehend the lyrics might then be able to reject the implied values. For example, half of a small sample of academically gifted 11- to 15-year-olds said that music had influenced how they thought about "an important topic," but 70% rejected lyrics that seemed to condone casual sex (Leming, 1987, p. 363). These teenagers might be relatively more "media-resistant." But a teenager's current area of development and stress could also lead him or her to be more susceptible to particular lyrics—for example, a teenager contemplating her first sexual intercourse might be more interested in sexy lyrics; a depressed teen might seek out songs of alienation (Christenson & Roberts, 1990).

Behavioral Impact of Lyrics. To date, *no* studies document a cause-and-effect relationship between sexy or violent lyrics and adverse behavioral effects (American Academy of Pediatrics, 1989; Hendren & Strasburger, 1993). However, four studies indicate that a preference for heavy metal music may be a significant *marker* for alienation, substance abuse, psychiatric disorders, or risk-taking behaviors during adolescence (King, 1988; Klein et al., 1993; Tanner, 1981; Weidinger & Demi, 1991):

1. In one early study, young adolescents who felt alienated from school life were more likely to prefer heavy metal music (Tanner, 1981).
2. Among teenagers in a hospital psychiatric unit, 59% of those admitted for chemical dependency rated heavy metal as their musical preference. Many of them were also involved in violence, stealing, and sexual activity. A second group of patients with psychiatric disturbances but less substance abuse rated heavy metal as their first choice 39% of the time. By contrast, only 17% of patients with primarily psychiatric disorders rated heavy metal as their top choice and were less likely to be involved in conduct-disordered behavior (King, 1988). A survey of 60 adolescents with dysfunctional psychosocial behaviors admitted to a different adolescent psychiatric unit found similar results (Weidinger & Demi, 1991).
3. A survey of more than 2,700 14- to 16-year-olds found that White male adolescents who reported engaging in five or more risk-taking behaviors (e.g., smoking cigarettes, drinking alcohol, cheating in school, having sex, cutting school, stealing money, smoking marijuana) were most likely to

name a heavy metal group as their favorite (Klein et al., 1993). The relative risk for engaging in five or more risky behaviors was 2.1 for girls and 1.6 for boys. Asking teenagers about their musical preferences could be a useful screening tool for primary care physicians and mental health professionals (Brown & Hendee, 1989).

Of course, until a longitudinal correlational study is performed, it is equally possible that alienation leads to a preference for heavy metal music rather than the reverse.

Conclusion. Overall, the research is incomplete on rock music and music lyrics, but if any conclusion can be drawn, it is that rock music has become increasingly more graphic in content but that different teenagers respond to lyrics differently, depending on their own unique psychological, social, and developmental makeup.

MUSIC VIDEOS AND MTV

As a visual medium, music videos are compelling. Not only do they possess the impact of ordinary television, but they could also be even more powerful. They represent a unique form of broadcast media that is impressionistic, nonlinear, and immensely popular with teenagers and preteenagers (Christenson & Roberts, 1990). Again, although no cause-and-effect studies exist, rock music videos seem capable of influencing teenagers' ideas about adult behavior and could potentially even modify their own behavior. Although adolescents seem to appreciate primarily the music, the addition of sexual or violent images seems to increase their excitement (Zillmann & Mundorf, 1987). There is concern that the power of the music and lyrics becomes magnified when visual images are added to them, increasing the risk of deleterious effects on young people (Hendren & Strasburger, 1993). Such concern seems justified, given that numerous studies have documented television's potential harmful effects in the areas of violence, smoking and drinking behavior, and healthy sexual development (Dietz & Strasburger, 1991; Strasburger & Comstock, 1993).

MTV is composed of performance videos, concept videos, and advertising. In a performance video, a musical performer or group sings the song in a concert or in a studio. Roughly half of all music videos are performance videos. A concept video consists of a story that goes along with the song, which may or may not add a plot to the lyrics.

Although performance videos can occasionally be outlandish (e.g., David Lee Roth's attire or his masturbating onstage with a huge inflatable phallus in the video "Yankee Rose"), no evidence suggests that such videos have demonstrable behavioral impact (American Academy of Pediatrics, 1989). Such depictions are roughly the equivalent of Elvis Presley gyrating his hips in the 1950s. Rather the concept videos have attracted much of the criticism for promoting violence, sexual promiscuity, and sexism. Concept videos are strongly male-oriented, and women are frequently worshipped as upper-class sex objects (e.g., Billy Joel's "Uptown Girl" or The Thunderbirds' "Wrap It Up"). Rock stars also serve as potential role models for impressionable children and young adolescents. When Madonna sings in "Papa Don't Preach" about keeping her baby while dancing around and looking like a thin Marilyn Monroe, it becomes that much more difficult to convince a pregnant 14-year-old that having a baby would be a severe hardship. One national columnist called it "a commercial for teenage pregnancy" (Goodman, 1986, p. A23). George Michael's "I Want Your Sex" combines striking sexual imagery with explicit lyrics describing how natural, how good, how wonderful sex is, and everyone should do it. It also includes the disclaimer that people should not have casual sex—they should explore monogamy. Of course, if the equivalent ploy were tried with cigarette labeling, the disclaimer might read: "Caution: Cigarettes may be hazardous to your health, but only if you smoke them."

Advertising on MTV parallels primetime advertising in that sex is used to sell every type of product except the one that teenagers could really benefit from—birth control (Strasburger, 1989a). Alcohol advertising is particularly prevalent. Occasionally, public service announcements discuss drugs or AIDS, but they are heavily outnumbered by beer commercials and ads that exploit female sexuality.

Consumption. Music videos have become a pervasive and influential form of consumer culture and have altered the television-viewing, music-listening, and record-buying habits of the young people who constitute its audience (Burnett, 1990). With 70% of American households receiving cable TV (Nielsen Media Research, 1993), most teenagers have access to MTV and may spend as many as 2 hours a day watching it (Sun & Lull, 1986), although most studies report closer to 30 to 60 minutes per day (Christenson & Roberts, 1990). MTV grows by more than five million households a year and is now available in 55 million homes (Polskin,

1991). It is also available in 40 countries overseas, reaching more than 194 million households (Polskin, 1991). As a commercial medium, its profits are projected to be nearly $100 million. The effects of MTV's advertising content are considerable and have been examined in detail elsewhere (see Strasburger, 1993b).

Content. A content analysis of concept music videos in 1985 showed that the characters portrayed were primarily white and male (Sherman & Dominick, 1986). Episodes of violence occurred in 57% of concept videos, with White males most likely to be the aggressors. Wrestling, punching, and grabbing were the most common forms of aggression and the outcome of the aggression was rarely shown. Sexual intimacy appeared in more than three quarters of the music videos studied and was more implied than overt. Half of all women were dressed provocatively and were often presented as upper-class sex objects. Furthermore, most of the violent videos also contained sexual imagery, usually involving violence against women. Another content analysis found that nearly 60% of concept videos contained sexual themes and more than half contained violence (Baxter, De Riemer, Landini, Leslie, & Singletary, 1985). In one analysis of sexism in rock videos, more than half portrayed women in a condescending manner (Vincent, Davis, & Bronszkowski, 1987). A more recent content analysis of 100 videos on MTV found that women are often portrayed as "bimbos" (Gow, 1993). At a time when an estimated 25% of American college women report having been raped or sexually assaulted (Hayes, 1987), such imagery seems unwise and unhealthy, even if direct behavioral consequences cannot be demonstrated scientifically.

Women have never fared very well on MTV, and that continues to be true in the 1990s. But more recently, music television has been more open to black performers, due in large part to the popularity of rap music (Leland, 1992). Videos aimed at a black audience also tend to be less antisocial and less negative than those targeting white viewers (Brown & Campbell, 1986).

Common themes in music videos include, in order of occurrence, visual abstraction (use of special effects to produce odd, unusual, or unexpected representations of reality), sex, dance, and violence or crime (Baxter et al., 1985). Music videos have also been shown to contain nihilistic images in 44% of the concept videos studied (Davis, 1985). This includes themes of destruction, death, ridicule of social institutions, and aggression against authority. As such, they seem to play on the presumably rebellious nature of the adolescent audience.

TABLE 6.2 Do Teenagers View Madonna's Music Videos Differently? Reactions to "Papa Don't Preach," by Race and Sex[a]

Primary Theme	Black Males (n = 28)	Black Females (n = 40)	White Males (n = 54)	White Females (n = 64)
Teen pregnancy	21	40	56	63
Boy/girl relationship	21	5	15	5
Father/daughter relationship	43	50	22	25
Independent girl making a decision	14	5	7	8
Part of theme deals with pregnancy	43	73	85	97

SOURCE: Brown and Schulze (1990). Oxford University Press. Reprinted with permission.

[a] Values are represented in percentages.

Unfortunately, there are no recent content analyses, nor are any analyses available that deal with health-related behaviors.

Comprehension. Music videos are more than just television plus music. They are self-reinforcing: If viewers hear a song after having seen the video version, they immediately "flashback" to the visual imagery in the video (Greenfield & Beagles-Roos, 1988). Obviously, what impact music videos have depends on how the viewer interprets them, and new evidence suggests that teenagers are a diverse group whose perceptions cannot always be predicted. For example, adolescent viewers of the Madonna video "Papa Don't Preach" differed in how they interpreted the story elements on the basis of sex and race (Brown & Schulze, 1990). Black viewers were almost twice as likely to say the video was a story of a father-daughter relationship, whereas white viewers were much more likely to say it was about teenage pregnancy. A similar study of Billy Ocean's video "Get Outta My Dreams, Get Into My Car" found that preteens tended to be very literal in interpreting the video (Christenson & Roberts, 1990). Some even said the video was about a man and his car, whereas 12-year-olds saw the video in more abstract terms, focusing on the relationship between the man and the woman. These studies suggest that both cognitive development and social background may play a significant role in how teenagers and preteens process music videos.

Watching music videos—particularly MTV—may differ from watching "regular television" or listening to the radio for the average adolescent. Music videos and MTV represent an entertaining diversion rather than a means of mood control or a social lubricant (Christenson & Roberts, 1990). If teenagers admit to learning anything from the medium, it is what's "hot" music- or fashion-wise rather than learning social values. MTV provides pictures of attractive people and, in many ways, functions as a style show. Yet 10- to 12-year-olds recognize that some of the sexual imagery and objectionable language may not be appropriate for them (Christenson & Roberts, 1990), so some value-laden material must be getting through as well.

Behavioral Effects. As with television in general, the amount of direct imitation of music videos or MTV is rare, but when it occurs, it makes national headlines. Such was the case when MTV's infamous show *Beavis and Butt-head* allegedly inspired a 5-year-old Moraine, Ohio, boy to set fire to his family's mobile home, killing his 2-year-old sister ("Mom Says MTV's 'Beavis' Led Son," 1993). The incident followed earlier reports that three girls in western Ohio had also started a fire while imitating a scene from the show (Hajari, 1993). Although *Beavis and Butt-head* is a cartoon, not a music video, it is prominently featured on MTV and much of the show involves the two main characters commenting on music videos. In response, MTV promised to delete all references to fire from future episodes and moved *Beavis and Butt-head* to a late-evening time slot (Hajari, 1993).

A handful of experimental studies have also been conducted. The concern that violent music videos might desensitize the viewer to violence has been born out in at least one study (Rehman & Reilly, 1985). Desensitization appears to operate on both a short- and long-term basis. In another study, 7th and 10th graders exposed to only 1 hour of selected music videos recorded from MTV were more likely to approve of premarital sex than were an adolescent control group (Greeson & Williams, 1986). In addition, the 10th graders exposed to the videos showed less disapproval of violence. In the most recent study, 46 inner-city black males from Wilmington, ages 11 to 16, were divided into three groups: The first group was exposed to a half hour of rap videos, complete with shootings and assaults; the second viewed nonviolent rap videos; and the third saw no videos. The teens were then given two different scenarios—one to test their propensity for violence, the other to determine their attitude about academics. Those who had viewed the violent videos were significantly more likely to condone violence in the theoretical scenario; and both groups of teens who viewed the rap videos were less likely to approve of high academic aspirations (Johnson, Jackson, & Gatto, in press).

Figure 6.1. Voluntary label affixed to record albums by record manufacturers.

Obviously, these are small, modest studies. Far more research is needed. But these studies are significant in paralleling the vast body of research done on media violence.

EFFECTS OF
PARENTAL ADVISORY LABELS

Since 1985, recording companies have been voluntarily adding parental advisory labels to record albums, tapes, or CDs that *they* judge to be violent, sexually explicit, or potentially offensive. Record companies are given the alternative of printing such lyrics on album jackets as consumer information for parents (Parents Music Resource Center, 1985). There has been a great deal of controversy about whether the labeling would result in the recordings becoming more or less appealing to adolescents.

As mentioned previously, several studies have found that most students cannot accurately describe the themes of their favorite songs and are usually unaware of the content or meanings of the lyrics. This raises the concern that labeling the album will call attention to the very themes that parent groups object to. Teenagers might then respond in one of two different ways:

avoiding the albums (the "tainted fruit" theory) or finding them more appealing (the "forbidden fruit" theory) (Christenson, 1992). In addition, printed lyrics on the jacket cover might make previously indecipherable lyrics easily accessible. (Imagine, for example, if the Kingsmen had *published* the lyrics of "Louie, Louie" on their album cover.) Only one experimental study has dealt with the issue of labeling. In it, young adolescents were asked to evaluate the same music, labeled and unlabeled (Christenson, 1992). The adolescents liked the labeled music less well, but the impact was limited. The adolescents reacted primarily to the music per se rather than the lyrics.

CONCLUSION

Despite the fact that rock 'n' roll is practically middle aged and MTV just turned 14 in 1995, research on popular music and music videos is in its infancy. There has been surprisingly little research about either, despite massive public concern about violent or sexually suggestive lyrics and videos. In addition, little attention has been paid to how these immensely popular media might be harnessed to provide prosocial or health-related messages. To date, no cause-and-effect studies exist to link either music or music videos with violent or sexually promiscuous behavior. For a small minority of teenagers, certain music may serve as a behavioral marker for psychological distress. The most important questions to ask before drawing any conclusions about the effects of rock music or music videos on an individual adolescent are: Which music? Which adolescents?

7

ADOLESCENTS AND
THE MEDIA: SOLUTIONS

What the culture at large needs to understand is that we're entering a completely
new realm where it's just not possible to control the information environment of
children. We need to find other ways of transmitting values.

Media critic Jonathan Katz
© Entertainment Weekly, Inc. Reprinted with permission.

A vast literature now exists that attests to the power of the media in influencing children's and adolescents' beliefs and, potentially, their behavior as
well. Unfortunately, American media currently contribute more to adverse
health outcomes than to positive or prosocial ones, but it does not have to
remain this way. The following are eight potential solutions that either
would improve the media or would immunize children against their harmful effects.

EIGHT SUGGESTIONS

1. The quality of programming for children and adolescents must be improved.

Although the Hollywood and New York creative communities see little
problem with the quality of their product, the research literature and most
parents disagree. American media are the most graphically violent and
sexually suggestive in the world. At present, the networks and studios have
virtually no incentive to create more educational and healthier programming, other than vague threats from Congress and the risk of noncompli-
ance with the Children's Television Act of 1990. Legislation requires local

TABLE 7.1 Joint Network Standards on TV Violence

Voluntary Limits on
- Gratuitous or excessive violence
- Glamorous depictions of violence
- Scenes showing excessive gore, pain, or physical suffering
- Scenes showing uses of force that are "on the whole" inappropriate for a home-viewing medium
- Replicable, unique, or "ingenious" depictions of inflicting pain or injury
- Portrayals of dangerous behavior or weapons that invite imitation by children
- In children's programs: realistic portrayals of violence that are unduly frightening
- Gratuitous depiction of animal abuse

Encourages
- Portrayal of the consequences of violence
- Scheduling all programs with regard for the likely composition of the intended audience

Urges Caution
- In stories and scenes showing children as victims
- In themes, plots, or scenes that mix sex and violence (e.g., rape)

SOURCE: News release, Senator Simon's office, Washington, DC, December 1992.

television stations to keep records of their efforts to provide "educational and informational" programming to children. Unfortunately, at present, stations are flaunting the will of Congress by claiming that programs such as *F-Troop* and *The Jetsons* satisfy the provision (*F-Troop* teaches teamwork; *The Jetsons* teaches children about the future!) (Flint, 1992). A more activist FCC could easily insist on proper compliance with the law (Aversa, 1994). But the creative community needs positive as well as negative incentives. Increased funding for children's TV could come either from a national tax on television sets annually (Britain funds the BBC with a $75/year/set tax) or from a 10% windfall profits tax on toy manufacturers who use cartoons to help sell their products (so-called program-length commercials). Sales of Mighty Morphin Power Rangers paraphernalia are expected to reach $1 billion in 1995, for example (Meyer & Tsiantar, 1994).

Other countries have given far higher priority to daily educational programming for children and adolescents—most notably, Great Britain and Japan. They have accomplished this by adequately funding their public television stations (Palmer, 1988). By contrast, there is not a single hour of daily educational programming for children on any of the four commercial networks in the United States (the last such show was *Captain Kangaroo*). The Corporation for Public Broadcasting, which controls PBS, is woefully underfunded and, of course, has to program for adults as well as children.

TABLE 7.2 Guide to Responsible Sexual Content in Television, Films, and Music

- Recognize sex as a healthy and natural part of life.
- Encourage parent-child discussions about sex.
- Discuss or show the consequences of unprotected sex.
- Show that not all relationships result in sex.
- Indicate that the use of contraceptives is essential.
- Avoid linking violence with sex.
- Depict rape as a crime of violence, not of passion.
- Recognize and respect the ability to say no.

SOURCE: Adapted from Center for Population Options (1987, pp. 9-11), with permission from Advocates for Youth (formerly The Center for Population Options).

Children and adolescents also deserve their own separate, commercial-free, educational channel—a Children's Television Network (Strasburger, 1988). If current predictions are correct (Waters & Beachy, 1993), 500 channels will be carried into households within the next decade using fiberoptic phone lines. If so, at least 10 to 20 such channels should be reserved for commercial-free, age-specific, educational programming for children and adolescents.

Broadcasters could also improve the current state of American programming by adhering to their own new voluntary guidelines regarding portrayals of violence and by adopting voluntary guidelines regarding portrayals of sex as well. Movie and record producers should consider such guidelines as well.

2. An improvement in programming must be accompanied by an improvement in the nature and rules of advertising.

As U.S. Supreme Court Justice Tom Clark once said, there is no war between the Constitution and common sense (Shiffrin, 1991). Compelling public health interests exist in protecting at least children and adolescents against the advertising of cigarettes and alcoholic beverages. Because advertising of these products represents *"commercial* speech," *it is not automatically protected under the First Amendment* (Ile & Krnoll, 1990; Shiffrin, 1993). In fact, commercial speech received *no* protection under the First Amendment until a court decision in 1976. Few industry spokesmen would challenge the constitutionality of the Public Health Act of 1969 that banned televised commercials for cigarettes. Furthermore, tobacco and alcohol advertising could be banned as being unfair and deceptive, given its appeal to underage drinkers and smokers.

The one significant drawback to a broadcast ban on alcohol advertising might be that from a public health viewpoint, it would be unwise if it eliminated effective counter-advertising (Atkin, 1993b; Grube & Wallack, 1994). One alternative would be to insist on tombstone advertising (i.e., ads that show the product only but do not depict the qualities that the drinker might acquire). Cigarette advertising has become so deceptive and harmful, however, that it justifies a ban in all media of all advertising, including promotional activities aimed at adolescents (Gostin & Brandt, 1993). Advertising of food products that are nutritionally unsound must also be severely curtailed and perhaps even banned on Saturday morning TV.

3. Birth control must be featured prominently in programming, and advertising for birth control products must be accepted, especially in programming popular with teenagers (e.g., MTV).

4. More research is needed in virtually every area of the media's impact on young people.

Although the violence research is conclusive, other research is only suggestive or incomplete. In addition, more information is needed about how to mediate harmful effects of the media. Specific studies that would be useful include

- A violence prevention project with a prominent media component
- Ongoing content analyses of violence and sex in television programming, movies, and rock music lyrics
- A longitudinal study of consumption of sexy media and subsequent sexual behavior
- A longitudinal study of the impact of rock music on adolescent behavior
- A content analysis of health-related behaviors in music videos
- An updated content analysis of MTV videos
- A longitudinal study of rock music's impact on affective states and suicidal intent
- Further research on the importance of individual responses to different media and why such variations occur

Of course, such research would require far more generous funding from government agencies and private foundations than currently exists.

In addition, since the 1982 National Institute of Mental Health report was issued, sufficient new data have been revealed to warrant a 1998 report on media and its impact on children and adolescents.

5. An increase in media literacy is vital to protect children and adolescents from harmful media influences.

Media literacy involves "demystifying" the media for young children. Parents can play a preeminent role in creating media-literate children, but only if they watch TV and movies with their children and explicitly discuss what is being viewed. Most studies suggest that media literacy can exert a protective effect against unhealthy attitudes learned from the media (Huston et al., 1992). For school-based programs, several different types of curricula have been developed. At Yale, the Singers have developed an eight-lesson critical viewing curriculum for 3rd through 5th graders that is designed to teach them how television programs are produced, how special effects are accomplished, how television reality differs from real-life reality, how stereotypes are portrayed on TV, and the unreality of TV violence (Singer, Zuckerman, & Singer, 1980). Dorr at UCLA has developed a similar curriculum (Dorr, Graves, & Phelps, 1980). Both have been field-tested extensively and successfully. In 1983, Huesmann and Eron developed a curriculum to counter some of the adverse effects of televised violence and successfully pilot-tested it. First and third graders who completed the program experienced changes in their attitudes about TV violence and in their own level of aggressive behavior as rated by their peers (Huesmann, Eron, Klein, Brice, & Fischer, 1983). More recently, the Center for Media and Values in Los Angeles has developed "Parenting in a TV Age," a four-session curriculum for parents, and "TV Alert: A Wakeup Guide to Television Literacy," an eight-lesson program for children (Center for Media Values, 1992). Also, Home Box Office and Consumer Reports have pioneered a series of shows, including *Buy Me That!* and *Buy Me That Too,* which teach children about television commercials and consumerism. Finally, the Singers have also developed an effective adolescent health education minicurriculum using five episodes of *Degrassi Junior High* with teens and preteens in Grades 5 through 8 (Singer & Singer, 1994).

Currently, this is an area of intensive research among communications specialists and may yield exciting new approaches in the 1990s for mediating the harmful effects of the media on children and adolescents.

6. Better understanding of the nature of the media is needed by parents and health professionals alike.

According to the media industry, if there are any untoward effects from TV, movies, and rock 'n' roll, it is only because children and adolescents are not being properly supervised and restricted. Given the penetration of media in American society, this argument is nearly laughable. And, of course, it would be far easier for parents to supervise their children if there were healthier programs from which to choose. Nevertheless, parents are guilty of using the TV as an electronic babysitter and underestimating the influence the media may be having on their children (Strasburger, 1993c). Likewise, health professionals could benefit from appreciating the negative and positive influences that the media may be having on their patients. Pediatricians and family practitioners, in particular, should take a careful television history when they see patients with any of the following problems (Dietz & Strasburger, 1991):

- Aggressive behavior in school
- Learning difficulties
- Obesity
- Depression
- Suicidal ideation

Specific counseling recommendations for families with children and teenagers include the following:

1. *Parents should be counseled to limit their children's TV viewing to no more than 1 hour per day.* Obviously, alternative activities must be provided and should be strongly encouraged.

2. *Parents need to monitor which shows their children and teens are watching.* Parents who continue to use the TV set as an electronic babysitter should at least carefully select prerecorded or rented tapes to be shown on the VCR rather than let their children play "channel roulette."

3. *Parents of teenagers need to realize that they can counteract the overly sexual or violent nature of much television programming, including MTV, but only if they watch such shows with their teens and explain their own views.* Clear explanations of parents' values and expectations—even if they are conservative ones—are useful and protective for teenagers against adverse media effects.

7. In addition to higher quality educational programming, more aggressive use of the media must be made for health campaigns and prosocial purposes.

Clearly, if the media can teach children that violence is acceptable or that drinking is normative behavior for teenagers, then they can also teach young people to respect their parents, to understand people of different racial or ethnic backgrounds, to avoid violence at all costs, and to avoid harming nature. Although using the media for prosocial purposes has some unpleasant, Orwellian possibilities, so little has been done in this regard that there seems little danger of abuse in the near future. In particular, radio remains nearly totally unexplored as a way of positively influencing teenagers.

To date, however, the success of public health media campaigns has been mixed. A $32 million AIDS campaign in Great Britain accomplished little more than raising general anxiety about AIDS, for example. Similarly, the Centers for Disease Control spent millions of dollars mailing an "Understanding AIDS" brochure to every household in the United States, but the brochure probably failed to reach those at the highest risk of contracting HIV infection (Brown & Walsh-Childers, 1994). However, a recent $2 million television and radio campaign in Vermont cut rates of teen smoking by 35% (Flynn et al., 1994).

Most campaigns subscribe to the "health belief model"—that is, if the individual knows the facts, he or she will choose a healthier alternative. Such a strategy is relatively easy: The "victim" is to blame. Meanwhile, advertisers continue to spend millions of dollars to encourage unhealthy consumption. To break this cycle, fundamental public policy changes are needed that will make it easier for people to adopt healthier behaviors (Brown & Walsh-Childers, 1994; Wallack et al., 1993).

8. Health professionals and parents need to engage vigorously in media advocacy.

Media advocacy is the "strategic use of mass media for advancing a social or public policy initiative" (National Cancer Institute, 1988). This involves refocusing public attention and debate on health issues, not individuals' foibles, as a matter of public policy. According to Wallack et al. (1993), current debates must be reframed. For example, tobacco manufacturers have deflected much attention by framing the debate about smoking as a free speech/individual freedom issue. The National Rifle Association has done likewise, despite the fact that federal courts, including the Supreme Court, have not interpreted the Second Amendment as guaranteeing everyone's right to own firearms (Asseo, 1993). Simply reclassifying guns as a consumer product would have a profound public health effect, especially because more stringent regulations currently govern the manufacture and sale of teddy bears than of guns (Sitton, 1994). Successful reframing involves exposing unethical industry practices rather than trying to improve individuals' behaviors by urging them to be healthy (Wallack et al., 1993).

CONCLUSION

In 1961, FCC Chairman Newton Minow shocked the broadcasting industry by calling American television "a vast wasteland" of game shows, murder, heroic bad guys, unbelievable good guys, blood, guts, and violent cartoons (Jones, 1994).

With thousands of research studies giving ample cause for concern, how much has really changed over the past 30 years? Good media (predominantly PBS on television; Disney and occasionally other studio films) continue to be drowned out by bad media. As the public health toll continues to climb (handgun deaths, injuries and deaths from drunken driving, teen pregnancies, HIV infection), the American public will look even more to the media to become part of the solution rather than part of the problem. In 1991, Minow added a sad epitaph to his original speech and said that 30 years ago, he was worried that his children would not benefit much from television; but today, he is afraid his grandchildren will be harmed by it.

It is an American tragedy that television and other media, which at times can be so astounding, so informative, and so entertaining, are allowed to produce programming whose primary objective is to make as much money as possible, with so little consideration of the nation's most valuable resource—its children and adolescents.

REFERENCES

Abramson, P. R., & Mechanic, M. B. (1983). Sex and the media: Three decades of best selling books and major motion pictures. *Archives of Sexual Behavior, 12,* 185-206.

Adriaenssens, E. E., Eggermont, E., Pyck, K., & Boeckx, W. (1988). The video invasion of rehabilitation. *Burns, 14,* 417-419.

Aitken, P. P., & Eadie, D. R. (1990). Reinforcing effects of cigarette advertising on under-age smoking. *British Journal of Addiction, 85,* 399-412.

Aitken, P. P., Eadie, D. R., Leathar, D. S., McNeill, R. E. J., & Scott, A. C. (1988). Television advertisements for alcoholic drinks do reinforce under-age drinking. *British Journal of Addiction, 83,* 1399-1419.

Alter, J. (1994, January 17). The power to change what's "cool." *Newsweek,* p. 23.

American Academy of Pediatrics, Committee on Adolescence. (1986). Sexuality, contraception, and the media. *Pediatrics, 78,* 535-536.

American Academy of Pediatrics, Committee on Adolescence. (1992). Firearms and adolescents. *Pediatrics, 89,* 784-787.

American Academy of Pediatrics, Committee on Communications. (1989). Impact of rock lyrics and music videos on children and youth. *Pediatrics, 83,* 314-315.

American Academy of Pediatrics, Committee on Communications. (1990). Children, adolescents, and television: Policy statement. *Pediatrics, 85,* 1019-1020. Elk Grove Village, IL: Author.

American Academy of Pediatrics, Committee on Substance Abuse. (1994). Tobacco-free environment: An imperative for the health of children and adolescents. *Pediatrics, 93,* 866-868.

Amos, A., Jacobson, B., & White, P. (1991). Cigarette advertising and coverage of smoking and health in British women's magazines. *Lancet, 337,* 93-96.

Anderson, C., & Ford, C. M. (1987). Affect of the game player: Short-term effects of highly and mildly aggressive video games. *Personality and Social Psychology Bulletin, 12,* 390-402.

Andison, F. S. (1977). TV violence and viewer aggressiveness: A cumulation of study results. *Public Opinion Quarterly, 41,* 324-331.

Armstrong, B. K., de Klerk, N. H., Shean, R. E., Dunn, D. A., & Dolin, P. J. (1990). Influence of education and advertising on the uptake of smoking by children. *Medical Journal of Australia, 152,* 117-124.

Arnett, J. (1991). Adolescents and heavy metal music: From the mouths of metalheads. *Youth & Society, 23,* 76-98.

Asseo, L. (1993, December 12). Courts don't favor right to bear arms. *Albuquerque Journal* [Associated Press].

Atkin, C. K. (1982). Television advertising and socialization to consumer roles. In D. Pearl, L. Bouthilet, & J. Lazar (Eds.), *Television and behavior: Ten years of scientific progress and implications for the eighties* (Vol. 2, pp. 191-200). Rockville, MD: National Institute of Mental Health.

Atkin, C. K. (1990). Effects of televised alcohol messages on teenage drinking patterns. *Journal of Adolescent Health Care, 11,* 10-24.

Atkin, C. K. (1993a). Alcohol advertising and adolescents. *Adolescent Medicine: State of the Art Reviews, 4,* 527-542.

Atkin, C. K. (1993b, Winter). On regulating broadcast alcohol advertising. *Journal of Broadcasting & Electronic Media,* 107-113.

Atkin, C. K. (in press). Survey and experimental research on effects of alcohol advertising. In S. Martin (Ed.), *Mass media and the use and abuse of alcohol.* Rockville, MD: National Institute on Alcohol Abuse and Alcoholism.

Atkin, C. K., & Block, M. (1983). Effectiveness of celebrity endorsers. *Journal of Advertising Research, 23,* 57-61.

Atkin, C. K., DeJong, W., & Wallack, L. (1992). *The influence of responsible drinking TV spots and automobile commercials on young drivers.* Washington, DC: AAA Foundation for Traffic Safety.

Atkin, C. K., Hocking, J., & Block, M. (1984). Teenage drinking: Does advertising make a difference? *Journal of Communication, 28,* 71-80.

Atkin, C. K., Neuendorf, K., & McDermott, S. (1983). The role of alcohol advertising in excessive and hazardous drinking. *Journal of Drug Education, 13,* 313-325.

Auletta, K. (1993). What won't they do? *The New Yorker, 69,* 45-63.

Aversa, J. (1994, June 29). FCC may boost regulations on kids educational shows. *Albuquerque Journal* [Associated Press].

Bailey, M. (1969). The women's magazine short-story heroine in 1957 and 1967. *Journalism Quarterly, 46,* 364-366.

Bailey, S. L. (1992). Adolescents' multisubstance use patterns: The role of heavy alcohol and cigarette use. *American Journal of Public Health, 82,* 1220-1224.

Bandura, A. (1963, October 22). What TV violence can do to your child. *Look,* pp. 46-52.

Bandura, A. (1965). Influence of models' reinforcement contingencies on the acquisition of imitative responses. *Journal of Personality and Social Psychology, 1,* 589-595.

Bandura, A. (1973). *Aggression: A social learning analysis.* Englewood Cliffs, NJ: Prentice Hall.

Bandura, A. (1977). *Social learning theory.* Englewood Cliffs, NJ: Prentice Hall.

Bandura, A. (1978). Social learning theory of aggression. *Journal of Communication, 28,* 12-29.

Bandura, A. (1994). Social cognitive theory of mass communication. In J. Bryant & D. Zillmann (Eds.), *Media effects: Advances in theory and research* (pp. 61-90). Hillsdale, NJ: Lawrence Erlbaum.

Bandura, A., Ross, D., & Ross, S. A. (1963). Imitation of film-mediated aggressive models. *Journal of Abnormal and Social Psychology, 66,* 3-11.

Baran, S. J. (1976a). How TV and film portrayals affect sexual satisfaction in college students. *Journalism Quarterly, 53,* 468-473.

Baran, S. J. (1976b). Sex on TV and adolescent sexual self-image. *Journal of Broadcasting, 20,* 61-68.

Baron, J. N., & Reiss, P. C. (1985). Reply to Phillips and Bollen. *American Sociological Review, 50,* 372-376.

Barry, M. (1991). The influence of the U.S. tobacco industry on the health, economy, and environment of developing countries. *New England Journal of Medicine, 324,* 917-920.

Bartecchi, C. D., MacKenzie, T. D., & Schrier, R. W. (1994). The human costs of tobacco use, part 1. *New England Journal of Medicine, 330,* 907-912.

Barton, R. (1989). Alcohol promotion on television. *World Health Forum, 10,* 181-185.

Bauman, K. E., LaPrelle, J., Brown, J. D., Koch, G. G., & Padgett, C. A. (1991). The influence of three mass media campaigns on variables related to adolescent cigarette smoking: Results of a field experiment. *American Journal of Public Health, 81,* 597-604.

Baxter, B. L., De Riemer, C., Landini, A., Leslie, L., & Singletary, M. W. (1985). A content analysis of music videos. *Journal of Broadcasting & Electronic Media, 29,* 333-340.

BBC bans beauty contest. (1985, June 30). *Parade Magazine.*

Belson, W. A. (1978). *Television violence and the adolescent boy.* Westmead, UK: Saxon House, Teakfield Ltd.

Berger, W. (1994, July 10). The amazing secrets of a television guru. *The New York Times, 2,* p. 1.

Berkowitz, L. (1962). *Aggression: A social psychological analysis.* New York: McGraw-Hill.

Berkowitz, L. (1964). The effects of observing violence. *Scientific American, 21,* 35-41.

Berkowitz, L. (1973). Words and symbols as stimuli to aggressive responses. In J. F. Knutson (Ed.), *Control of aggression: Implications from basic research.* Chicago: Aldine-Atherton.

Berkowitz, L. (1984). Some effects of thoughts on anti- and prosocial influences of media events: A cognitive-neoassociation analysis. *Psychological Bulletin, 95,* 410-427.

Berkowitz, L., & Alioto, J. T. (1973). The meaning of an observed event as a determinant of aggressive consequences. *Journal of Personality and Social Psychology, 28,* 206-217.

Berkowitz, L., & Geen, R. G. (1966). Film violence and the cue properties of available targets. *Journal of Personality and Social Psychology, 3,* 525-530.

Berkowitz, L., & Geen, R. G. (1967). Stimulus qualities of the target of aggression: A further study. *Journal of Personality and Social Psychology, 5,* 364-368.

Berkowitz, L., & Rawlings, E. (1963). Effects of film violence on inhibitions against subsequent aggression. *Journal of Abnormal and Social Psychology, 66,* 405-412.

Blum, A. (1991). The Marlboro Grand Prix—Circumvention of the television ban on tobacco advertising. *New England Journal of Medicine, 324,* 913-917.

Braverman, P. K., & Strasburger, V. C. (1993). Adolescent sexual activity. *Clinical Pediatrics, 32,* 658-668.

Breed, W., & De Foe, J. R. (1981). The portrayal of the drinking process on prime-time television. *Journal of Communication, 31,* 58-67.

Breed, W., & De Foe, J. R. (1982). Effecting media change: The role of cooperative consultation on alcohol topics. *Journal of Communication, 32,* 88-99.

Breed, W., & De Foe, J. R. (1983). Cigarette smoking on television: 1950-1982 [letter]. *New England Journal of Medicine, 309,* 617.

Breed, W., & De Foe, J. R. (1984). Drinking and smoking on television, 1950-1982. *Journal of Public Health Policy, 31,* 257-270.

Brent, D. A., Perper, J. A., Allman, C. J., Moritz, G. M., Wartella, M. E., & Zelenak, J. P. (1991). The presence and accessibility of firearms in the homes of adolescent suicides: A case-control study. *Journal of the American Medical Association, 266,* 2989-2995.

Brent, D. A., Perper, J. A., Moritz, G., Baugher, M., Schweers, J., & Roth, C. (1993). Firearms and adolescent suicide: A community case-control study. *American Journal of Diseases of Children, 147,* 1066-1071.

Broder, S. (1992). Cigarette advertising and corporate responsibility. *Journal of the American Medical Association, 268,* 782-783.

Brown, D., & Bryant, J. (1989). Uses of pornography. In D. Zillmann & J. Bryant (Eds.), *Pornography: Research advances and policy considerations* (pp. 3-24). Hillsdale, NJ: Lawrence Erlbaum.

Brown, E. F., & Hendee, W. R. (1989). Adolescents and their music: Insights into the health of adolescents. *Journal of the American Medical Association, 262,* 1659-1663.

Brown, J., & Campbell, K. (1986). Race and gender in music videos: The same beat but a different drummer. *Journal of Communication, 36,* 94-106.

Brown, J. D., Childers, K. W., & Waszak, C. S. (1990). Television and adolescent sexuality. *Journal of Adolescent Health, 11,* 62-70.

Brown, J. D., & Newcomer, S. F. (1991). Television viewing and adolescents' sexual behavior. *Journal of Homosexuality, 21,* 77-91.

Brown, J. D., & Schulze, L. (1990). The effects of race, gender, and fandom on audience interpretations of Madonna's music videos. *Journal of Communication, 40,* 88-102.

Brown, J. D., & Walsh-Childers, K. (1994). Effects of media on personal and public health. In J. Bryant & D. Zillmann (Eds.), *Media effects: Advances in theory and research* (pp. 389-415). Hillsdale, NJ: Lawrence Erlbaum.

Bryant, J., & Anderson, D. R. (1983). *Children's understanding of television.* New York: Academic Press.

Bryant, J., & Rockwell, S. C. (1994). Effects of massive exposure to sexually-oriented primetime television programming on adolescents' moral judgment. In D. Zillmann, J. Bryant & A. C. Huston (Eds.), *Media, children, and the family: Social, scientific, psychodynamic, and clinical perspectives* (pp. 183-195). Hillsdale, NJ: Lawrence Erlbaum.

Buchanan, D. R., & Lev, J. (1990). *Beer and fast cars: How brewers target blue-collar youth through motor sport sponsorships.* Washington, DC: AAA Foundation for Traffic Safety.

Buerkel-Rothfuss, N. L., & Mayes, S. (1981). Soap opera viewing: The cultivation effect. *Journal of Communication, 31,* 108-115.

Burke, R., & Grinder, R. (1966). Personality-oriented themes and listening patterns in teen-age music and their relation to certain academic and peer variables. *School Review, 74,* 196-211.

Burnett, R. (1990). From a whisper to a scream: Music video and cultural form. In K. Roe & U. Carlsson (Eds.), *Popular music research* (pp. 21-27). Goteborg, Sweden: Nordicom-Sweden.

Canonzoneri, V. (1984, January 28). TV's feminine mistake. *TV Guide,* pp. 14-15.

Carlsson-Paige, N., & Levin, D. E. (1991, Winter). The subversion of healthy development and play: Teachers' reactions to the teenage mutant ninja turtles. *Day Care and Early Education,* pp. 14-20.

Carveth, R., & Alexander, A. (1985). Soap opera viewing motivation and the cultivation process. *Journal of Broadcasting and Electronic Media, 29,* 259-273.

Caucus for Producers, Writers, and Directors. (1983). *We've done some thinking.* Santa Monica, CA: Television Academy of Arts and Sciences.

Center for Media Values. (1992). Media literacy. *Media & Values, 59/60,* 41-42.

Center for Population Options. (1987, March/April). Adolescents sexuality in the media. *SIECUS Report*, 9-110.

Center for Population Options. (1993). *Fact sheet: Adolescents, HIV and other sexually transmitted diseases*. Washington, DC: Author.

Center for Science in the Public Interest. (1988). *Kids are as aware of booze as president, survey finds* [News release]. Washington, DC: Author.

Center for Science in the Public Interest. (1992, November). *Survey of advertising on children's TV.* Washington, DC: Author.

Centers for Disease Control. (1987). Youth suicide in the United States, 1970-1980. *Morbidity & Mortality Weekly Report, 36*, 87-89.

Centers for Disease Control. (1989). Results from the national adolescent student health survey. *Morbidity & Mortality Weekly Report, 38*, 147-150.

Centers for Disease Control. (1990). Cigarette advertising—United States, 1988. *Morbidity & Mortality Weekly Report, 39*, 261-265.

Centers for Disease Control. (1992a). Accessibility of cigarettes to youths aged 12-17 years—United States, 1989. *Morbidity & Mortality Weekly Report, 41*, 485-488.

Centers for Disease Control. (1992b). Comparison of the cigarette brand preferences of adult and teenaged smokers—United States, 1989, and 10 U.S. communities, 1988 and 1990. *Morbidity & Mortality Weekly Report, 41*, 169-181.

Centers for Disease Control. (1992c). Firearm-related deaths—Louisiana and Texas, 1970-1990. *Morbidity & Mortality Weekly Report, 41*, 213-221.

Centers for Disease Control. (1993). Sexual risk behaviors of STD clinic patients before and after Earvin "Magic" Johnson's HIV-infection announcement—Maryland, 1991-1992. *Morbidity & Mortality Weekly Report, 42*, 45-48.

Centers for Disease Control. (1994a). Deaths resulting from firearm- and motor-vehicle-related injuries—United States, 1968-1991. *Morbidity & Mortality Weekly Report, 43*, 37-42.

Centers for Disease Control. (1994b). Medical-care expenditures attributable to cigarette smoking—United States, 1993. *Morbidity & Mortality Weekly Report, 43*, 469-472.

Centers for Disease Control. (1994c). *Preventing tobacco use among young people: A report of the Surgeon General.* Atlanta, GA: U.S. Department of Health and Human Services.

Centerwall, B. S. (1992a). Children, television, and violence. In D. F. Schwarz (Ed.), *Children and violence* (pp. 87-97). Columbus, OH: Ross Laboratories.

Centerwall, B. S. (1992b). Television and violence: The scale of the problem and where to go from here. *Journal of the American Medical Association, 267*, 3059-3063.

Christenson, P. (1992). The effects of parental advisory labels on adolescent music preferences. *Journal of Communication, 42*, 106-113.

Christenson, P. G., & Roberts, D. F. (1990). *Popular music in early adolescence.* Washington, DC: Carnegie Council on Adolescent Development. *) from p. 87*

Christoffel, K. K. (1991). Toward reducing pediatric injuries from firearms: Charting a legislative and regulatory course. *Pediatrics, 88*, 294-305.

Christoffel, K. K., & Cristoffel, T. (1986). Handguns as a pediatric problem. *Pediatric Emergency Care, 2*, 343-349.

Cline, V. B. (1994). Pornography effects: Empirical and clinical evidence. In D. Zillmann, J. Bryant, & A. C. Huston (Eds.), *Media, children, and the family: Social, scientific, psychodynamic, and clinical perspectives* (pp. 229-247). Hillsdale, NJ: Lawrence Erlbaum.

Cline, V. B., Croft, R. B., & Courrier, S. (1973). Desensitization of children to television violence. *Journal of Personality and Social Psychology, 35*, 450-458.

106   ADOLESCENTS AND THE MEDIA

Coleman, J. (1978). Current contradictions in adolescent theory. *Journal of Youth and Adolescence, 7,* 1-11.

Coles, R., & Stokes, G. (1985). *Sex and the American teenager.* New York: Harper and Row.

Comstock, G. (1986). Television and film violence. In S. J. Apter & A. P. Goldstein (Eds.), *Youth violence: Programs and prospects* (pp. 178-218). Elmsford, NY: Pergamon.

Comstock, G. (1991). *Television and the American child.* San Diego: Academic Press.

Comstock, G., & Strasburger, V. C. (1990). Deceptive appearances: Television violence and aggressive behavior—An introduction. *Journal of Adolescent Health, 11,* 31-44.

Comstock, G. C., & Strasburger, V. C. (1993). Media violence: Q & A. *Adolescent Medicine: State of the Art Reviews, 4,* 495-509.

Cooper, J., & Mackie, D. (1986). Video games and aggression in children. *Journal of Applied Social Psychology, 16,* 726-744.

Corder-Bolz, C. (1981). Television and adolescents' sexual behavior. *Sex Education Coalition News, 3,* p. 40.

Courtright, J. A., & Baran, S. J. (1980). The acquisition of sexual information by young people. *Journalism Quarterly, 57,* 107-114.

Creasey, G. L., & Myers, B. J. (1986). Video games and children: Effects on leisure activities, schoolwork, and peer involvement. *Merrill-Palmer Quarterly, 32,* 251-262.

Daven, J., O'Conner, J. F., & Briggs, R. (1976). The consequences of imitative behavior in children: The "Evel Knievel syndrome." *Pediatrics, 57,* 418-419.

David, A. (1993, May 2). Screen stats. *Entertainment Weekly,* p. 67.

Davidson, L. E., Rosenberg, M. L., Mercy, J. A., Franklin, J., & Simmons, J. T. (1989). An epidemiologic study of risk factors in two teenage suicide clusters. *Journal of the American Medical Association, 262,* 2687-2692.

Davidson, O. G. (1993). *Under fire: The NRA and the battle for gun control.* New York: Holt, Rinehart & Winston.

Davis, S. (1985, Summer). Pop lyrics: A mirror and molder of society. *Et Cetra,* pp. 167-169.

Dawson, D. A. (1986). The effects of sex education on adolescent behavior. *Family Planning Perspectives, 18,* 162-170.

De Foe, J. R., & Breed, W. (1988). Youth and alcohol in television stories, with suggestions to the industry for alternative portrayals. *Adolescence, 23,* 533-550.

DeJong, W. (1995). *"Old Joe Camel," editor-in-chief: KKR, RJR Nabisco, and the Weekly Reader Corporation.* Manuscript submitted for publication.

Denisoff, R. S., & Levine, M. H. (1971). The popular protest song: The case of "Eve of Destruction." *Public Opinion Quarterly, 35,* 119-124.

Dietz, W. H., Jr. (1993). Television, obesity, and eating disorders. *Adolescent Medicine: State of the Art Reviews, 4,* 543-549.

Dietz, W. H., Jr., & Gortmaker, S. L. (1985). Do we fatten our children at the television set? Obesity and television viewing in children and adolescents. *Pediatrics, 75,* 807-812.

Dietz, W. H., Jr., & Gortmaker, S. L. (1993). TV or not TV: Fat is the question. *Pediatrics, 91,* 499-501.

Dietz, W. H., & Strasburger, V. C. (1991). Children, adolescents, and television. *Current Problems in Pediatrics, 21,* 8-31.

DiFranza, J. R., Richards, J. W., Jr., Paulman, P. M., Fletcher, C., & Jaffe, R. D. (1992). Tobacco: Promotion and smoking [letter]. *Journal of the American Medical Association, 267,* 3282-3284.

DiFranza, J. R., Richards, J. W., Paulman, P. M., Wolf-Gillespie, N., Fletcher, C., Jaffe, R. D., & Murray, D. (1991). RJR Nabisco's cartoon camel promotes Camel cigarettes to children. *Journal of the American Medical Association, 266,* 3149-3153.

DiFranza, J. R., & Tye, J. B. (1990). Who profits from tobacco sales to children? *Journal of the American Medical Association, 263,* 2784-2787.

Dominick, J. R. (1984). Videogames, television violence, and aggression in teenagers. *Journal of Communication, 34,* 136-147.

Dominick, J. R., & Greenberg, B. S. (1972). Attitudes toward violence: The interaction of television exposure, family attitudes and social class. In G. A. Comstock & E. A. Rubinstein (Eds.), *Television and social behavior: Vol. 3. Television and adolescent aggressiveness* (pp. 314-335). Washington, DC: U.S. Government Printing Office.

Donnerstein, E. (1984). Pornography: Its effect on violence against women. In N. M. Malamuth & E. Donnerstein (Eds.), *Pornography and sexual aggression* (pp. 53-81). Orlando, FL: Academic Press.

Donnerstein, E., Linz, D., & Penrod, S. (1987). *The question of pornography: Research findings and policy implications.* New York: Free Press.

Dorr, A., Graves, S. B., & Phelps, E. (1980). Television literacy for young children. *Journal of Communication, 30,* 71-83.

Drabman, R. S., & Thomas, M. H. (1974). Does media violence increase children's toleration of real-life aggression? *Developmental Psychology, 10,* 418-421.

Ebert, R. (1993, June 6). [Review of the film *The Last Action Hero*]. *Siskel and Ebert.* [Television program].

Egli, E. A., & Myers, L. S. (1984). The role of video game playing in adolescent life: Is there reason to be concerned? *Bulletin of the Psychonomic Society, 22,* 309-312.

Elkind, D. (1984, November/December). Teenage thinking: Implications for health care. *Pediatric Nursing,* pp. 383-385.

Elkind, D. (1993). *Parenting your teenager in the 90's* (pp. 72, 384). Rosemont, NJ: Modern Learning Press.

Ellerbee, L. (1986). *And so it goes—Adventures in television* (p. 34). New York: G. P. Putnam.

Ellis, G. T., & Sekrya, F. (1972). The effect of aggressive cartoons on the behavior of first grade children. *Journal of Psychology, 81,* 37-43.

Entertainers have the last laugh, pocket millions of fans' dollars. (1990, October 7). *Atlanta Journal,* p. A3.

Eron, L. R. (1993). *The problem of media violence and children's behavior.* New York: Henry Frank Guggenheim Foundation.

Eron, L. R. (1995, February). Media violence. *Pediatric Annals.*

Fabes, R. A., & Strouse, J. S. (1984). Youth's perceptions of models of sexuality: Implications for sexuality education. *Journal of Sex Education and Therapy, 10,* 33-37.

Fabes, R. A., & Strouse, J. S. (1987). Perceptions of responsible and irresponsible models of sexuality: A correlational study. *Journal of Sex Research, 23,* 70-84.

Families sue band over sons' suicides. (1990, July 16). *Albuquerque Journal,* p. C12.

Federman, J. (1993). *Film and television ratings: An international assessment.* Studio City, CA: Mediascope.

Fedler, F., Hall, J., & Tanzi, L. (1982). Popular songs emphasize sex, deemphasize romance. *Mass Communication Review, 9,* 10-15.

Feingold, M., & Johnson, G. T. (1977). Television violence—Reactions from physicians, advertisers, and the networks. *New England Journal of Medicine, 296,* 424-427.

Feldman, W., Feldman, E., & Goodman, J. T. (1988). Culture versus biology: Children's attitudes towards thinness and fitness. *Pediatrics, 81,* 190-194.

Feshbach, S., & Singer, R. D. (1971). *Television and aggression: An experimental field study.* San Francisco: Jossey-Bass.

Fingerhut, L. A., & Kleinman, J. C. (1990). International and interstate comparisons of homicide among young males. *Journal of the American Medical Association, 263,* 3292-3295.

Fischer, P. M., Richards, J. W., Jr., Berman, E. J., & Krugman, D. M. (1989). Recall and eye tracking study of adolescents viewing tobacco advertisements. *Journal of the American Medical Association, 261,* 84-89.

Fischer, P. M., Schwart, M. P., Richards, J. W., Goldstein, A. O., & Rojas, T. H. (1991). Brand logo recognition by children aged 3 to 6 years: Mickey Mouse and Old Joe the Camel. *Journal of the American Medical Association, 266,* 3145-3153.

Flint, J. (1992, October 5). Study slams broadcasters' kids act compliance. *Broadcasting,* pp. 40-41.

Flynn, B. S., Worden, J. K., Secker-Walker, R. H., Pirie, P. L., Badger, G. J., Carpenter, J. H., & Geller, B. M. (1994). Mass media and school interventions for cigarette smoking prevention: Effects 2 years after completion. *American Journal of Public Health, 84,* 1148-1150.

Freuh, T., & McGhee, P. (1975). Traditional sex-role development and amount of time watching television. *Developmental Psychology, 11,* 109.

Friedman, H., Termini, S., & Washington, R. (1977). The effectiveness of advertisements utilizing four types of endorsers. *Journal of Advertising, 6,* 22-24.

Frith, S. (1992). The industrialization of popular music. In J. Lull (Ed.), *Popular music and communication* (2nd ed., pp. 49-74). Newbury Park, CA: Sage.

Funk, J. (1992). Video games: Benign or malignant? *Journal of Developmental and Behavioral Pediatrics, 13,* 53-54.

Funk, J. (1993a). Reevaluating the impact of video games. *Clinical Pediatrics, 32,* 86-90.

Funk, J. (1993b). Video games. *Adolescent Medicine: State of the Art Reviews, 4,* 589-598.

Furstenberg, F. F., Moore, K. A., & Peterson, J. L. (1985). Sex education and sexual experience among adolescents. *American Journal of Public Health, 75,* 1331-1332.

Gadow, K. D., & Sprafkin, J. (1989). Field experiments of television violence with children: Evidence for an experimental toxin? *Pediatrics, 83,* 399-405.

Gagnon, J. H., & Simon, W. (1987). The sexual scripting of oral genital contacts. *Archives of Sexual Behavior, 16,* 1-25.

Geen, R. G. (1994). Television and aggression: Recent developments in research and theory. In D. Zillmann, J. Bryant, & A. C. Huston (Eds.), *Media, children, and the family: Social, scientific, psychodynamic, and clinical perspectives* (pp. 151-162). Hillsdale, NJ: Lawrence Erlbaum.

Geen, R. G., & Stoner, D. (1972). Context effects in observed violence. *Journal of Personality and Social Psychology, 25,* 145-150.

Gerbner, G. (1985). Children's television: A national disgrace. *Pediatric Annals, 14,* 822-827.

Gerbner, G. (1990). Stories that hurt: Tobacco, alcohol, and other drugs in the mass media. In H. Resnik (Ed.), *Youth and drugs: Society's mixed messages* (OSAP Prevention Monograph-6, pp. 53-129). Rockville, MD: Office for Substance Abuse Prevention.

Gerbner, G. (1992). Society's storyteller: How television creates the myths by which we live. *Media & Values, 59/60,* 8-9.

Gerbner, G. (1993, June). *Women and minorities on television: A study in casting and fate.* Report presented to the Screen Actors Guild and the American Federation of Radio and Television Artists, Annenberg School for Communication, Philadelphia.

Gerbner, G., Gross, L., Morgan, M., & Signorielli, N. (1980a). Health and medicine on television. *New England Journal of Medicine, 305,* 901-904.

Gerbner, G., Gross, L., Morgan, M., & Signorielli, N. (1980b). The "mainstreaming" of America: Violence profile no. 11. *Journal of Communication, 30,* 10-29.

Gerbner, G., Gross, L., Morgan, M., & Signorielli, N. (1986). The dynamics of the cultivation process. In J. Bryant & D. Zillmann (Eds.), *Perspectives on media effects* (pp. 17-48). Hillsdale, NJ: Lawrence Erlbaum.

Gerbner, G., Gross, L., Morgan, M., & Signorielli, N. (1994). Growing up with television: The cultivation perspective. In J. Bryant & D. Zillmann (Eds.), *Media effects: Advances in theory and research* (pp. 17-41). Hillsdale, NJ: Lawrence Erlbaum.

Gerbner, G., Morgan, M., & Signorielli, N. (1982). Programming health portrayals: What viewers see, say and do. In D. Pearl, L. Bouthilet, & J. Lazar (Eds.), *Television and behavior: Ten years of scientific progress and implications for the eighties* (Vol. 2, pp. 291-307). Rockville, MD: National Institute of Mental Health.

Gerbner, G., Morgan, M., & Signorielli, N. (1994). *Television violence profile no. 16.* Philadelphia: Annenberg School for Communication.

Giles, J., & Fleming, C. (1993, June 28). See kids' flix make big bucks. *Newsweek,* p. 66.

Gilligan, C. (1990). *Making connections: The relational world of adolescent girls at Emma Willard School.* Cambridge, MA: Harvard University Press.

Goldberg, M. (1987, November 28). TV has done more to contain AIDS than any other single factor. *TV Guide,* pp. 5-6.

Goldstein, A. O., Fischer, P. M., Richards, J. W., Jr., & Creten, D. (1987). Relationship between high school student smoking and recognition of cigarette advertisements. *Journal of Pediatrics, 110,* 488-491.

Goodman, E. (1986, September 20). Commercial for teen-age pregnancy. *Washington Post,* p. A23.

Gortmaker, S. L., Must, A., Perrin, J. M., Sobol, A. M., & Dietz, W. H. (1993). Social and economic consequences of overweight in adolescence and young adulthood. *New England Journal of Medicine, 329,* 1008-1012.

Gostin, L. O., & Brandt, A. M. (1993). Criteria for evaluating a ban on the advertisement of cigarettes. *Journal of the American Medical Association, 269,* 904-909.

Gottlieb, A., Pope, S. K., Rickert, V. I., & Hardin, B. H. (1993). Patterns of smokeless tobacco use by young adolescents. *Pediatrics, 91,* 75-78.

Gould, M. S., & Davidson, L. (1988). Suicide contagion among adolescents. *Advances in Adolescent Mental Health, 3,* 29-59.

Gould, M. S., & Shaffer, D. (1986). The impact of suicide in television movies. *New England Journal of Medicine, 315,* 690-694.

Gould, M. S., Shaffer, D., & Kleinman, M. (1988). The impact of suicide in television movies: Replication and commentary. *Suicide and Life-Threatening Behavior, 18,* 90-99.

Gow, J. (1993). *Gender roles in popular music videos: MTV's "top 100 of all time."* Paper presented at the 1993 Popular Culture Association/American Culture Association convention, New Orleans, LA.

Graf, W. D., Chatrian, G.-E., Glass, S. T., & Knauss, T. A. (1994). Video game-related seizures: A report on 10 patients and a review of the literature. *Pediatrics, 93,* 551-556.

Graham, L., & Hamdan, L. (1987). *Youth trends: Capturing the $200 billion youth market.* New York: St. Martin's.

Greenberg, B. S. (1975). British children and televised violence. *Public Opinion Quarterly, 38,* 531-547.

Greenberg, B. S. (1982). Television and role socialization: An overview. In D. Pearl, L. Bouthilet, & J. Lazar (Eds.), *Television and behavior: Ten years of scientific progress and implications for the eighties* (Vol. 2, pp. 179-190). Rockville, MD: National Institute of Mental Health.

Greenberg, B. S. (1988). Some uncommon television images and the drench hypothesis. In S. Oskamp (Ed.), *Applied social psychology annual: Vol. 8. Television as a social issue* (pp. 88-102). Beverly Hills, CA: Sage.

Greenberg, B. S. (1994). Content trends in media sex. In D. Zillmann, J. Bryant, & A. C. Huston (Eds.), *Media, children, and the family: Social scientific, psychodynamic, and clinical perspectives* (pp. 165-182). Hillsdale, NJ: Lawrence Erlbaum.

Greenberg, B. S., Abelman, R., & Neuendorf, K. (1981). Sex on the soap operas: Afternoon delight. *Journal of Communication, 31,* 83-89.

Greenberg, B. S., Brown, J. D., & Buerkel-Rothfuss, N. (1993). *Media, sex and the adolescent.* Cresskill, NJ: Hampton.

Greenberg, B. S., Linsangan, R. L., Soderman, A., Heeter, C., Lin, C., Stanley, C., & Siemicki, M. (1987). *Adolescents and their exposure to television and movie sex* (Project CAST Report No. 4). East Lansing: Michigan State University, Department of Telecommunications.

Greenberg, B. S., Stanley, C., Siemicki, M., Heeter, C., Soderman, A., & Linsangan, R. (1986). *Sex content on soaps and primetime television series viewed by adolescents* (Project CAST Report No. 3). East Lansing: Michigan State University, Department of Telecommunications.

Greene, J. S., & Asher, I. (1982). Electronic games [letter]. *Journal of the American Medical Association, 248,* 1308.

Greenfield, P., & Beagles-Roos, J. (1988). Television vs. radio: The cognitive impact on different socio-economic and ethnic groups. *Journal of Communication, 38,* 71-92.

Greenfield, P. M., Bruzzone, L., Koyamatsu, K., Satuloff, W., Nixon, K., Brodie, M., & Kingsdale, D. (1987). What is rock music doing to the minds of our youth? A first experimental look at the effects of rock music lyrics and music videos. *Journal of Early Adolescence, 7,* 315-329.

Greeson, L. E., & Williams, R. A. (1986). Social implications of music videos for youth: An analysis of the contents and effects of MTV. *Youth & Society, 18,* 177-189.

Griffith, J. L., Voloschin, P., Gibb, G. D., & Bailey, J. R. (1983). Differences in eye-hand coordination of video-game users and non-users. *Perceptual and Motor Skills, 57,* 155-158.

Grossberg, L. (1992). Rock and roll in search of an audience. In J. Lull (Ed.), *Popular music and communication* (2nd ed., pp. 152-175). Newbury Park, CA: Sage.

Grube, J. W. (1993). Alcohol portrayals and alcohol advertising on television. *Alcohol Health & Research World, 17,* 61-66.

Grube, J. W., & Wallack, L. (1994). Television beer advertising and drinking knowledge, beliefs, and intentions among school children. *American Journal of Public Health, 84,* 254-259.

Gunter, B. (1994). The question of media violence. In J. Bryant & D. Zillmann (Eds.), *Media effects: Advances in theory and research* (pp. 163-211). Hillsdale, NJ: Lawrence Erlbaum.

Haffner, D. W., & Kelly, M. (1987, March/April). Adolescent sexuality in the media. *SIECUS Report*, pp. 9-12.

Hajari, N. (1993, October 22). Playing with fire. *Entertainment Weekly*, pp. 6-7.

Hanratty, M. A., O'Neal, E., & Sulzer, J. L. (1972). The effect of frustration upon imitation of aggression. *Journal of Personality and Social Psychology, 21,* 30-34.

Harris, L., & Associates. (1985). *Public attitudes about sex education, family planning and abortion in the United States*. New York: Planned Parenthood Federation of America.

Harris, L., & Associates. (1986). *American teens speak: Sex, myths, TV and birth control*. New York: Planned Parenthood Federation of America.

Harris, L., & Associates. (1987). *Attitudes about television, sex and contraception advertising*. New York: Planned Parenthood Federation of America.

Harris, L., & Associates. (1988). *Sexual material on American network television during the 1987-88 season*. New York: Planned Parenthood Federation of America.

Harris, R. J. (1994). The impact of sexually explicit media. In J. Bryant & D. Zillmann (Eds.), *Media effects: Advances in theory and research* (pp. 247-272). Hillsdale, NJ: Lawrence Erlbaum.

Hawkins, R. P., & Pingree, S. (1982). Television's influence on social reality. In D. Pearl, L. Bouthilet, & J. Lazar (Eds.), *Television and behavior: Ten years of scientific progress and implications for the eighties* (Vol. 2, pp. 224-247). Rockville, MD: National Institute of Mental Health.

Hayes, C. D. (Ed.). (1987). *Risking the future: Adolescent sexuality, pregnancy, and childbearing* (Vol. 1). Washington, DC: National Academic Press.

Hazan, A. R., Lipton, H. L., & Glantz, S. A. (1994). Popular films do not reflect current tobacco use. *American Journal of Public Health, 84,* 998-1000.

Healy, J. M. (1990). *Endangered minds: Why our children don't think*. New York: Simon & Schuster.

Hearold, S. (1986). A synthesis of 1045 effects of television on social behavior. In G. Comstock (Ed.), *Public communication and behavior* (Vol. 1, pp. 65-133). New York: Academic Press.

Hendren, R. L., & Strasburger, V. C. (1993). Rock music and music videos. *Adolescent Medicine: State of the Art Reviews, 4,* 577-587.

Hennigan, K. M., Heath, L., Wharton, J. D., Del Rosario, M. L., Cook, T. D., & Calder, B. J. (1982). Impact of the introduction of television on crime in the United States: Empirical findings and theoretical implications. *Journal of Personality and Social Psychology, 42,* 461-477.

Herold, E. S., & Foster, M. E. (1975). Changing sexual references in mass circulation magazines. *The Family Coordinator, 24,* 21-25.

Hibbard, R. A., Brack, C. J., Rauch, S., & Orr, D. P. (1988). Abuse, feelings, and health behaviors in a student population. *American Journal of Diseases of Children, 142,* 326-330.

Hicks, D. J. (1965). Imitation and retention of film-mediated aggressive peer and adult models. *Journal of Personality and Social Psychology, 2,* 97-100.

Hicks, D. J. (1968). Short- and long-term retention of affectively varied modeled behavior. *Psychonomic Science, 11,* 369-370.

Horn, J. (1994, January 7). Al Gore, cyberpunks mingle in TV summit. *Albuquerque Journal* [Associated Press].

Huesmann, L. R. (1982). Television violence and aggressive behavior. In D. Pearl, L. Bouthilet, & J. Lazar (Eds.), *Television and behavior: Ten years of scientific progress and implications for the eighties* (Vol. 2, pp. 126-137). Rockville, MD: National Institute of Mental Health.

Huesmann, L. R. (1986). Psychological processes promoting the relation between exposure to media violence and aggressive behavior by the viewer. *Journal of Social Issues, 42,* 125-139.

Huesmann, L. R., & Eron, L. D. (Eds.). (1986). *Television and the aggressive child: A cross-national comparison.* Hillsdale, NJ: Lawrence Erlbaum.

Huesmann, L. R., Eron, L. D., Klein, R., Brice, P., & Fischer, R. (1983). Mitigating the imitation of aggressive behaviors by changing children's attitudes about media violence. *Journal of Personality and Social Psychology, 44,* 899-910.

Huesmann, L. R., Eron, L. D., Lefkowitz, M. M., & Walder, L. O. (1984). Stability of aggression over time and generations. *Developmental Psychology, 20,* 1120-1134.

Huston, A. C., Donnerstein, E., Fairchild, H., Feshbach, N. D., Katz, P. A., Murray, J. P., Rubinstein, E. A., Wilcox, B. L., & Zuckerman, D. (1992). *Big world, small screen: The role of television in American society.* Lincoln: University of Nebraska Press.

Ile, M. L., & Krnoll, L. A. (1990). Tobacco advertising and the First Amendment. *Journal of the American Medical Association, 264,* 1593-1594.

Iwao, S., Pool, I. S., & Hagiwara, S. (1981). Japanese and U.S. media: Some cross-cultural insights into TV violence. *Journal of Communication, 31,* 28-36.

Jacobson, M. F., & Collins, R. (1985, March 10). There's too much harm to let beer, wine ads continue. *Los Angeles Times.*

James, C. (1993, October 24). If Simon says, "Lie down in the road," should you? *New York Times.*

Jeffrey, D. B., McLellarn, R. W., & Fox, D. T. (1982). The development of children's eating habits: The role of television commercials. *Health Education Quarterly, 9,* 78-93.

Jo, E., & Berkowitz, L. (1994). A priming effect analysis of media influences: An update. In J. Bryant & D. Zillmann (Eds.), *Media effects: Advances in theory and research* (pp. 43-60). Hillsdale, NJ: Lawrence Erlbaum.

Johnson, I. (1993, December 20). Networks more than just surviving. *The Baltimore Sun.*

Johnson, J. D., Jackson, L. A., & Gatto, L. (in press). Violent attitudes and deferred academic aspirations: Deleterious effects of exposure to rap music. *Basic and Applied Social Psychology.*

Johnston, L., Bachman, J., & O'Malley, P. (1994). 1993 monitoring the future survey. Ann Arbor, MI: University of Michigan.

Jones, D. (1988, April 13). We rely on TV or AIDS information. *USA Today.*

Jones, E. F., Forrest, J. D., Goldman, N., Henshaw, S. K., Lincoln, R., Rosoff, J. I., Westoff, C. F., & Wulf, D. (1985). Teenage pregnancy in developed countries: Determinants and policy implications. *Family Planning Perspectives, 17,* 53-63.

Jones, E. F., Forrest, J. D., Henshaw, S. K., Silverman, J., & Torres, A. (1988). Unintended pregnancy, contraceptive practice and family planning services in developed countries. *Family Planning Perspectives, 20,* 53-67.

Jones, T. (1994, May 15). "Vast wasteland" author still displeased with TV. *Chicago Tribune,* p. C5.

Kalichman, S. C., & Hunter, T. L. (1992). The disclosure of celebrity HIV infection: Its effects on public attitudes. *American Journal of Public Health, 82,* 1374-1376.

Kaufman, L. (1980). Prime-time nutrition. *Journal of Communication, 30,* 37-45.

Kegeles, S. M., Adler, N. E., & Irwin, C. E. (1988). Sexually active adolescents and condoms: Changes over one year in knowledge, attitude and use. *American Journal of Public Health, 78,* 460-461.

Kellerman, A. L., & Reay, D. T. (1986). Protection or peril? An analysis of a national random survey of gun owners. *New England Journal of Medicine, 314,* 1557-1560.

Kellerman, A. L., Rivara, F. P., Rushforth, N. B., Banton, J. G., Reay, D. T., Francisco, J. T., Locci, A. B., Prodzinski, J., Hackman, B. B., & Somes, G. (1993). Gun ownership as a risk factor for homicide in the home. *New England Journal of Medicine, 329,* 1084-1091.

Kellerman, A. L., Rivara, F. P., Somes, G., Reay, D. T., Francisco, J., Banton, J. G., Prodzinski, J., Fligner, C. L., & Hackman, B. B. (1992). Suicide in the home in relation to gun ownership. *New England Journal of Medicine, 327,* 467-472.

Kenrick, D. T., & Guttieres, S. E. (1980). Contrast effects and judgments of physical attractiveness: When beauty becomes a social problem. *Journal of Personality and Social Psychology, 38,* 131-140.

Kessler, L. (1989). Women's magazines coverage of smoking related health hazards. *Journalism Quarterly, 66,* 316-323.

Kilbourne, J. (1990, October/November). The case against advertising of "legal" drugs. *Adolescent Counselor,* pp. 24-39.

Kilbourne, J. (1991). Deadly persuasion: 7 myths alcohol advertisers want you to believe. *Media & Values, 54/55,* 10-12.

Kilbourne, J. (1993). Killing us softly: Gender roles in advertising. *Adolescent Medicine: State of the Art Reviews, 4,* 635-649.

Kilbourne, J. E., Painton, S., & Ridley, D. (1985). The effect of sexual embedding on responses to magazine advertisements. *Journal of Advertising, 14,* 48-56.

Killen, J. D., Taylor, C. B., Teleh, M. J., Saylor, K. E., Maron, D. J., & Robinson, T. N. (1986). Self-induced vomiting and laxative and diuretic use among teenagers. *Journal of the American Medical Association, 255,* 1447-1449.

Kinder, M. (1991). *Playing with power in movies, television, and video games.* Berkeley: University of California Press.

King, P. (1988). Heavy metal music and drug abuse in adolescents. *Postgraduate Medicine, 83,* 295-302.

Kirby, D. (1980). The effects of school sex education programs: A review of the literature. *Journal of School Health, 50,* 559-563.

Klein, J. D., Brown, J. D., Childers, K. W., Oliveri, J., Porter, C., & Dykers, C. (1993). Adolescents' risky behavior and mass media use. *Pediatrics, 92,* 24-31.

Klesges, R. C., Shelton, M. L., & Klesges, L. M. (1993). Effects of television on metabolic rate: Potential implications for childhood obesity. *Pediatrics, 91,* 281-286.

Klitzner, M., Gruenewald, P. J., & Bamberger, E. (1991). Cigarette advertising and adolescent experimentation with smoking. *British Journal of Addiction, 86,* 287-298.

Koenig, R. L. (1992, September 4). Brewhaha: "Youth-oriented" beer ads opposed. *St. Louis Post Dispatch,* p. 1.

Kohn, P. M., & Smart, R. G. (1984). The impact of television advertising on alcohol consumption: An experiment. *Journal of Studies on Alcohol, 45,* 295-301.

Kohn, P. M., & Smart, R. G. (1987). Wine, women, suspiciousness and advertising. *Journal of Studies on Alcohol, 48,* 161-166.

Kolko, D. J., & Rickard-Figueroa, J. L. (1985). Effects of video games on the adverse corollaries of chemotherapy in pediatric oncology patients: A single-case analysis. *Journal of Consulting and Clinical Psychology, 53,* 223-228.

Kotch, J. B., Coulter, M. L., & Lipsitz, A. (1986). Does televised drinking influence children's attitudes toward alcohol? *Addictive Behaviors, 11,* 67-70.

Ku, L., Sonenstein, F. L., & Pleck, J. H. (1993). Young men's risk behaviors for HIV infection and sexually transmitted diseases, 1988 through 1991. *American Journal of Public Health, 83,* 1609-1615.

Kuczmarski, R. J., Flegal, K. M., Campbell, S. M., & Johnson, C. L. (1994). Increasing prevalence of overweight among U.S. adults. *Journal of the American Medical Association, 272,* 205-211.

Kunkel, D., & Gantz, W. (1991). *Television advertising to children: Message content in 1990.* Report presented to the Children's Advertising Review Unit of the National Advertising Division, Council of Better Business Bureaus, Inc., Bloomington, Indiana University.

Larson, R., & Kubey, R. (1983). Television and music: Contrasting media in adolescent life. *Youth & Society, 15,* 13-31.

Laugesen, M., & Meads, C. (1991). Tobacco advertising restrictions, price, income and tobacco consumption in OECD countries, 1960-1986. *British Journal of Addiction, 86,* 1343-1354.

LaVoie, J., & Collins, B. (1975). Effects of youth culture music on high school students' academic performance. *Journal of Youth and Adolescence, 4,* 57-65.

Lefkowitz, M. M., Eron, L. D., Walder, L. O., & Huesmann, L. R. (1972). Television violence and child aggression: A follow-up study. In G. A. Comstock & E. A. Rubinstein (Eds.), *Television and social behavior: Vol. 3. Television and adolescent aggressiveness* (pp. 35-135). Washington, DC: U.S. Government Printing Office.

Leland, J. (1992, June 29). Rap and rage. *Newsweek,* pp. 46-52.

Leland, J. (1993, November 29). Criminal records: Gangsta rap and the culture of violence. *Newsweek,* pp. 60-64.

Leming, J. (1987). Rock music and the socialization of moral values in early adolescence. *Youth & Society, 18,* 363-383.

Leo, J. (1993, October 20). '90s advertisements portray women with "attitude." *Albuquerque Journal,* p. A11.

Leyens, J. P., & Camino, L. (1974). The effects of repeated exposure to film violence on aggressiveness and social structures. In J. DeWit & W. P. Hartup (Eds.), *Determinants and origins of aggressive behavior.* The Hague, The Netherlands: Mouton.

Leyens, J. P., Camino, L., Parke, R. D., & Berkowitz, L. (1975). Effects of movie violence on aggression in a field setting as a function of group dominance and cohesion. *Journal of Personality and Social Psychology, 32,* 346-360.

Lieberman, L. R., & Orlandi, M. A. (1987). Alcohol advertising and adolescent drinking. *Alcohol, Health & Research World, 11,* 30-45.

Liebert, R. M., & Sprafkin, J. (1988). *The early window—Effects of television on children and youth* (3rd ed.). New York: Pergamon.

Linz, D., & Donnerstein, E. (1988). The methods and merits of pornography research. *Journal of Communication, 38,* 180-184.

Linz, D., & Malamuth, N. (1993). *Pornography.* Newbury Park, CA: Sage.

Lipman, J. (1991, August 21). Alcohol firms put off public. *Wall Street Journal*, p. B1.

Loftin, C., McDowall, D., Wiersema, B., & Cottey, T. J. (1991). Effects of restrictive licensing of handguns on homicide and suicide in the District of Columbia. *New England Journal of Medicine, 325,* 1615-1620.

Lovaas, O. I. (1961). Effect of exposure to symbolic aggression on aggressive behavior. *Child Development, 32,* 37-44.

Lowery, S. A. (1980). Soap and booze in the afternoon: An analysis of the portrayal of alcohol use in daytime serials. *Journal of Studies on Alcohol, 41,* 829-838.

Lowry, D. T., Love, G., & Kirby, M. (1987). Sex on the soap operas: Patterns of intimacy. *Journal of Communication, 31,* 90-96.

Lowry, D. T., & Towles, D. E. (1989). Soap opera portrayals of sex, contraception, and sexually transmitted diseases. *Journal of Communication, 39,* 76-83.

Loye, D., Gorney, R., & Steele, G. (1977). Effects of television: An experimental field study. *Journal of Communication, 27,* 206-216.

Lull, J. (1987). Listeners' communicative uses of popular music. In J. Lull (Ed.), *Popular music and communication* (pp. 140-174). Newbury Park, CA: Sage.

Lyons, J. S., Anderson, R. L., & Larson, D. B. (1994). A systematic review of the effects of aggressive and nonaggressive pornography. In D. Zillmann, J. Bryant, & A. C. Huston (Eds.), *Media, children, and the family: Social scientific, psychodynamic, and clinical perspectives* (pp. 271-310). Hillsdale, NJ: Lawrence Erlbaum.

MacKenzie, T. D., Bartecchi, C. D., & Schrier, R. W. (1994). The human costs of tobacco use, part 2. *New England Journal of Medicine, 30,* 975-980.

MacKinnon, D. P., Pentz, M. A., & Stacy, A. W. (1993). The alcohol warning label and adolescents: The first year. *American Journal of Public Health, 83,* 585-587.

MacVean, M. (1993, May 12). Food marketers aiming at kids. *Albuquerque Journal* [Associated Press].

Madden, P. A., & Grube, J. W. (1994). The frequency and nature of alcohol and tobacco advertising in televised sports, 1990 through 1992. *American Journal of Public Health, 84,* 297-299.

Maeda, Y., Kurokawa, T., Sahamota, K., Kitamoto, I., Veda, K., & Tashima, S. (1990). Electroclinical study of video-game epilepsy. *Developmental Medicine and Child Neurology, 32,* 493-500.

Malamuth, N. M. (1993). Pornography's impact on male adolescents. *Adolescent Medicine: State of the Art Reviews, 4,* 563-576.

Maloney, M. J., McGuire, J., Daniels, S. R., & Specker, B. (1989). Dieting behavior and eating attitudes in children. *Pediatrics, 84,* 482-489.

Marsh, D. (1993). *Louie Louie.* New York: Hyperion.

Marshall, E. (1991). Sullivan overrules NIH on sex survey. *Science, 253,* 502.

Marsiglio, W., & Mott, F. L. (1986). The impact of sex education on sexual activity, contraceptive use and premarital pregnancy among American teenagers. *Family Planning Perspectives, 18,* 151-161.

Martin, J. R., Sklar, D. P., & McFeeley, P. (1991). Accidental firearm fatalities among New Mexico children. *Annals of Emergency Medicine, 20,* 58-61.

McGinnis, J. M., & Foege, W. H. (1993). Actual causes of death in the United States. *Journal of the American Medical Association, 270,* 2207-2212.

McIntyre, J. J., & Teevan, J. J., Jr. (1972). Television violence and deviant behavior. In G. A. Comstock & E. A. Rubinstein (Eds.), *Television and social behavior: Vol. 3. Television and adolescent aggressiveness* (pp. 383-435). Washington, DC: U.S. Government Printing Office.

McLeod, J. M., Atkin, C. K., & Chaffee, S. H. (1972a). Adolescents, parents, and television use: Adolescent self-report measures from Maryland and Wisconsin samples. In G. A. Comstock & E. A. Rubinstein (Eds.), *Television and social behavior: Vol. 3. Television and adolescent aggressiveness* (pp. 173-238). Washington, DC: U.S. Government Printing Office.

McLeod, J. M., Atkin, C. K., & Chaffee, S. H. (1972b). Self-report and other-report measures from the Wisconsin sample. In G. A. Comstock & E. A. Rubinstein (Eds.), *Television and social behavior: Vol. 3. Television and adolescent aggressiveness* (pp. 239-313). Washington, DC: U.S. Government Printing Office.

Medved, M. (1992). *Hollywood vs. America.* New York: HarperCollins.

Mehrabian, A., & Wixen, W. J. (1986). Preferences for individual video games as a function of their emotional effects on players. *Journal of Applied Social Psychology, 16,* 3-15.

Meyer, M., & Tsiantar, D. (1994, August 8). Ninja turtles, eat our dust. *Newsweek,* pp. 34-35.

Milavsky, J. R., Kessler, R., Stipp, H. H., & Rubens, W. S. (1982). *Television and aggression: A panel study.* New York: Academic Press.

Milgram, S., & Shotland, R. L. (1973). *Television and antisocial behavior: A field experiment.* New York: Academic Press.

Mintz, M. (1991, May 6). Marketing tobacco to children. *The Nation,* pp. 577-596.

Mom says MTV's "Beavis" led son to start fatal fire. (1993, October 17). *Albuquerque Journal.*

Moog, C. (1991). The selling of addiction to women. *Media & Values, 54/55,* 20-22.

Moran, T. (1985, August 12-19). Sounds of sex. *The New Republic,* pp. 14-16.

Morgan, M. (1987). Television, sex role attitudes, and sex role behavior. *Journal of Early Adolescence, 7,* 269-282.

Morganstern, H. (1982). Use of ecologic analysis in epidemiologic research. *American Journal of Public Health, 72,* 1336-1344.

Morganstern, J. (1972, February 14). The new violence. *Newsweek.*

Moses, N., Banilivy, M. M., & Lifshitz, F. (1989). Fear of obesity among adolescent girls. *Pediatrics, 83,* 393-398.

Mullen, B. (1989). *Advanced basic meta-analysis.* Hillsdale, NJ: Lawrence Erlbaum.

Murchek, P. (1994, January 6). Dear Abby: Reduce abortion need. *Albuquerque Journal,* p. B2.

Murray, J. P., & Kippax, S. (1978). Children's social behavior in three towns with differing television experience. *Journal of Communication, 28,* 19-29.

Myerowitz, J. (1982). *No sense of place: The impact of electronic media on social behavior.* New York: Oxford University Press.

Myers, M. G., & Brown, S. A. (1994). Smoking and health in substance-abusing adolescents: A two-year follow-up study. *Pediatrics, 93,* 561-566.

National Cancer Institute. (1988). *Media strategies for smoking control* (NIH Publication No. 89-3013). Washington, DC: U.S. Government Printing Office.

National Council for Families & Television. (1994). *Report on the industry-wide leadership conference on violence in television programming.* Beverly Hills, CA: Author.

National Science Foundation. (1977). *Research on the effects of television advertising on children: A review of the literature and recommendations for future research.* Washington, DC: Author.

Nielsen Media Research. (1993). *1992-1993 report on television.* New York: Author.

Offer, D., Ostrov, E., & Howard, K. I. (1989). Adolescence: What is normal? *American Journal of Diseases of Children, 143,* 731-736.

Orlandi, M. A., Lieberman, L. R., & Schinke, S. P. (1989). The effects of alcohol and tobacco advertising on adolescents. In M. A. Orlandi, L. R. Lieberman, & S. P. Schinke (Eds.), *Perspectives on adolescent drug use* (pp. 77-97). Binghamton, NY: Haworth.

Paik, H. J. (1991). *The effects of television violence on aggressive behavior: A meta-analysis.* Unpublished doctoral dissertation, Syracuse University, NY.

Painter, K. (1994, January 5). AIDS ads get less "timid." *USA Today,* p. 1A.

Palmer, E. L. (1988). *Television and America's children.* New York: Oxford University Press.

Pareles, J. (1990, June 17). Rap: Slick, violent, nasty, and, maybe, hopeful. *New York Times,* p. 4.

Parents Music Resource Center. (1985). *PMRC, PTA, and RIAA agree on record lyrics identification* [PMRC press release]. Arlington, VA: Author.

Partnership for a Drug-Free America. (1992). *1987-1991 survey findings.* New York: Author.

Pearl, D. (1982). *Television and behavior: Ten years of scientific progress and implications for the eighties* (Vol. 1, DHHS Publication No. ADM 82-1195). Washington, DC: U.S. Government Printing Office.

Pearl, D., Bouthilet, L., & Lazar, J. (Eds.). (1982). *Television and behavior: Ten years of scientific progress and implications for the eighties* (Vol. 1, summary report). Rockville, MD: National Institute of Mental Health.

Peirce, K. (1993). Socialization of teenage girls through teen-magazine fiction: The making of a new woman or an old lady? *Sex Roles, 29,* 59-68.

Peterson, J. L., Moore, K. A., & Furstenberg, F. F., Jr. (1991). Television viewing and early initiation of sexual intercourse: Is there a link? *Journal of Homosexuality, 21,* 93-118.

Peterson, R. A., & Kahn, J. R. (1984, August 26). *Media preferences of sexually active teens.* Paper presented at the meeting of the American Psychological Association, Toronto, Canada.

Peto, R., Lopez, A. D., Boreham, J., Thun, M., & Heath, C., Jr. (1992). Mortality from tobacco in developed countries: Indirect estimation from national vital statistics. *Lancet, 339,* 1268-1278.

Phillips, D. P., & Carstensen, L. L. (1986). Clustering of teenage suicides after television news stories about suicide. *New England Journal of Medicine, 315,* 685-689.

Phillips, D. P., Carstensen, L. L., & Paight, D. J. (1989). Effects of mass media news stories on suicide, with new evidence on the role of story content. In C. R. Pfeffer (Ed.), *Suicide among youth: Perspectives on risk and prevention* (pp. 101-116). Washington, DC: American Psychiatric Press.

Phillips, D. P., & Paight, B. A. (1987). The impact of televised movies about suicide: A replicative study. *New England Journal of Medicine, 317,* 809-811.

Piaget, J. (1972). Intellectual evolution from adolescence to adulthood. *Human Development, 15,* 1-12.

Pierce, J. P., Gilpin, E., Burns, D. M., Whalen, E., Rosbrook, B., Shopland, D., & Johnson, M. (1991). Does tobacco advertising target young people to start smoking? *Journal of the American Medical Association, 266,* 3154-3158.

Pierce, J. P., Lee, L., & Gilpin, E. A. (1994). Smoking initiation by adolescent girls, 1944 through 1988: An association with targeted advertising. *Journal of the American Medical Association, 271,* 608-611.

Pierce, J. P., Macaskill, P., & Hill, D. (1990). Long-term effectiveness of mass media led antismoking campaigns in Australia. *American Journal of Public Health, 80,* 565-569.

Plagens, P., Miller, M., Foote, D., & Yoffe, E. (1991, April 1). Violence in our culture. *Newsweek,* pp. 46-52.

Pollay, R. W. (1991). Cigarettes under fire: Blowing away the PR smoke screen. *Media & Values, 54/55,* 13-16.

Polskin, H. (1991, August 3). MTV at 10. *TV Guide,* pp. 4-8.

Postman, N. (1985). *Amusing ourselves to death.* New York: Penguin.

Postman, N., Nystrom, C., Strate, L., & Weingartner, C. (1988). *Myths, men, & beer: An analysis of beer commercials on broadcast television, 1987.* Washington, DC: AAA Foundation for Traffic Safety.

Prinsky, L. E., & Rosenbaum, J. L. (1987). "Leer-ics" or lyrics: Teenage impressions of rock 'n' roll. *Youth & Society, 18,* 384-397.

Provenzo, E. F., Jr. (1991). *Video kids: Making sense of Nintendo.* Cambridge, MA: Harvard University Press.

Quigley, E. V. (1987, October 30). ABC, CBS, and NBC refuse to air "pill" commercials. *Los Angeles Times.*

Rehman, S. N., & Reilly, S. S. (1985). Music videos: A new dimension of televised violence. *The Pennsylvania Speech Communication Annual, 41,* 61-64.

Reichelt, P. A. (1978). Changes in sexual behavior among unmarried teenage women utilizing oral contraception. *Journal of Population Behavior, 1,* 59-68.

Reis, E. C., Duggan, A. K., Adger, H., & DeAngelis, C. (1992). The impact of anti-drug advertising on youth substance abuse [abstract]. *American Journal of Diseases of Children, 146,* 519.

Roberts, E. (1983). Teens, sexuality and sex: Our mixed messages. *Television & Children, 6,* 9-12.

Roberts, E. J. (1982). Television and sexual learning in childhood. In D. Pearl, L. Bouthilet, & J. Lazar (Eds.), *Television and behavior: Ten years of scientific progress and implications for the eighties* (Vol. 2, pp. 209-223). Rockville, MD: National Institute of Mental Health.

Robinson, J. P., & Bachman, J. G. (1972). Television viewing habits and aggression. In G. A. Comstock & E. A. Rubinstein (Eds.), *Television and social behavior: Vol. 3. Television and adolescent aggressiveness* (pp. 372-382). Washington, DC: U.S. Government Printing Office.

Robinson, T. N., Hammer, L. D., Killen, J. D., Kraemer, H. C., Wilson, D. M., Hayward, C., & Taylor, C. B. (1993). Does television viewing increase obesity and reduce physical activity? Cross-sectional and longitudinal analyses among adolescent girls. *Pediatrics, 91,* 273-280.

Roe, K. (1984). *Youth and music in Sweden: Results from a longitudinal study of teenagers' media use.* (Media Panel Rep. No. 32). Lund, Sweden: Sociologiska Institutionen.

Roe, K. (1990). Adolescent music use: A structural-cultural approach. In K. Roe & U. Carlsson (Eds.), *Popular music research* (pp. 41-52). Goteborg, Sweden: Nordicom-Sweden.

Romelsjo, A. (1987). Decline in alcohol-related problems in Sweden greatest among young people. *British Journal of Addiction, 82,* 1111-1124.

Rosen, D. S., Xiangdong, M., Blum, R. W. (1990). Adolescent health: Current trends and critical issues. *Adolescent Medicine: State of the Art Reviews, 1,* 15-31.

Rosenberg, M. L., Mercy, J. A., & Houk, V. N. (1991). Guns and adolescent suicides. *Journal of the American Medical Association, 266,* 3030.

Rothenberg, G. (1988, August 31). TV industry plans fight against drunken driving. *New York Times.*

Rothenberg, M. B. (1975). Effect of television violence on children and youth. *Journal of the American Medical Association, 234,* 1043-1046.

Rushforth, N. B., Hirsch, C. S., Ford, A. B., & Adelson, L. (1975). Accidental firearm fatalities in a metropolitan county: 1958-1973. *American Journal of Epidemiology, 100,* 499-505.

Samuelson, R. J. (1991, August 19). The end of advertising? *Newsweek,* p. 40.

Savitsky, J. C., Rogers, R. W., Izard, C. E., & Liebert, R. M. (1971). Role of frustration and anger in the imitation of filmed aggression against a human victim. *Psychological Reports, 29,* 807-810.

Scanlan, C. (1993, June 27). Teen suicides rise in homes with guns. *Albuquerque Journal,* p. A19.

Schetky, D. (1985). Children and handguns: A public health concern. *American Journal of Diseases of Children, 139,* 229-231.

Schonberg, S. K. (Ed.). (1988). *Substance abuse: A guide for health professionals.* Elk Grove Village, IL: American Academy of Pediatrics.

Schramm, W., Lyle, J., & Parker, E. B. (1961). *Television in the lives of our children.* Stanford, CA: Stanford University Press.

Schutte, N. S., Malouff, J. M., Post-Gorden, J. C., & Rodasta, A. L. (1988). Effects of playing videogames on children's aggressive and other behaviors. *Journal of Applied Social Psychology, 18,* 454-460.

Schydlower, M., & Shafer, M.-A. (Eds.). (1990). AIDS and other STDs. *Adolescent Medicine: State of the Art Reviews, 1,* 409-647.

Scott, J. E. (1986). An updated longitudinal content analysis of sex references in mass circulation magazines. *Journal of Sex Research, 22,* 385-392.

Segal, K. R., & Dietz, W. H. (1991). Physiologic responses to playing a video game. *American Journal of Diseases of Children, 131,* 1034-1036.

Sege, R., & Dietz, W. (1994). Television viewing and violence in children: The pediatrician as agent for change. *Pediatrics, 94* (Supplement), 600-607.

Selling to children. (1990, August). *Consumer Reports,* pp. 518-521.

Selverstone, R. (1992). Sexuality education for adolescents. *Adolescent Medicine: State of the Art Reviews, 3,* 195-205.

Sexuality Study Group Summary. (1990). Study group report on the impact of television on adolescent views of sexuality. *Journal of Adolescent Health, 11,* 71-75.

Shaffer, D., & Fisher, P. (1981). The epidemiology of suicide in children and young adolescents. *Journal of the American Academy of Child Psychiatry, 20,* 545-565.

Shaffer, D., Garland, A., Gould, M., Fisher, P., & Trautman, P. (1988). Preventing teenage suicide: A critical review. *Journal of the American Academy of Child Psychiatry, 27,* 675-687.

Shales, T. (1989, March 23). CBS' new Monday sitcoms misbegotten, doggedly unoriginal. *Albuquerque Journal.*

Shales, T. (1993, December 19). Sunday night sleaze parade on Fox. *Albuquerque Journal.*

Sherman, B. L., & Dominick, J. R. (1986). Violence and sex in music videos: TV and rock 'n' roll. *Journal of Communication, 36,* 79-93.

Shiffrin, S. H. (1991). How free is commercial speech? *Media & Values, 54/55,* 8-9.

Shiffrin, S. H. (1993). Alcohol and cigarette advertising: A legal primer. *Adolescent Medicine: State of the Art Reviews, 4,* 623-634.

from
p. 46

Signorielli, N. (1990). Television and health: Images and impact. In C. Atkin & L. Wallack (Eds.), *Mass communication and public health* (pp. 96-113). Newbury Park, CA: Sage.

Signorielli, N. (1993). Sex roles and stereotyping on television. *Adolescent Medicine: State of the Art Reviews, 4,* 551-561.

Signorielli, N., & Lears, M. (1992). Television and children's conceptions of nutrition: Unhealthy messages. *Health Communication, 4,* 245-257.

Silverman-Watkins, L. T. (1983). Sex in the contemporary media. In J. Q. Maddock, G. Neubeck, & M. B. Sussman (Eds.), *Human sexuality and the family* (pp. 125-140). New York: Haworth.

Silvern, S. B., & Williamson, P. A. (1987). The effects of video game play on young children's aggression, fantasy, and prosocial behavior. *Journal of Applied Developmental Psychology, 8,* 453-462.

Singer, D. (1985a). Alcohol, television, and teenagers. *Pediatrics, 76*(4, Pt. 2), 668-674.

Singer, D. G. (1985b). Does violent television produce aggressive children? *Pediatric Annals, 14,* 804-810.

Singer, D. G. (1989). Children, adolescents, and television 1989. I. Television violence: A critique. *Pediatrics, 83,* 445-446.

Singer, D. G., & Singer, J. L. (1994). Evaluating the classroom viewing of a television series, *Degrassi Junior High.* In D. Zillmann, J. Bryant, & A. C. Huston (Eds.), *Media, children, and the family: Social, scientific, psychodynamic, and clinical perspectives* (pp. 97-115). Hillsdale, NJ: Lawrence Erlbaum.

Singer, D. G., Zuckerman, D. M., & Singer, J. L. (1980). Helping elementary school children learn about TV. *Journal of Communication, 30,* 84-93.

Singer, J. L., & Singer, D. G. (1980). Television viewing and aggressive behavior in preschool children: A field study. *Annals of the Academy of Science, 347,* 289-303.

Singer, J. L., & Singer, D. G. (1981). *Television, imagination, and aggression: A study of preschoolers.* Hillsdale, NJ: Lawrence Erlbaum.

Singer, J. L., Singer, D. G., & Rapaczynski, W. (1984). Family patterns and television viewing as predictors of children's beliefs and aggression. *Journal of Communication, 34,* 73-89.

Sitton, L. (1994, May 15). Labeling gun a consumer product stirs safety debate. *Albuquerque Journal,* p. B5.

Sloan, J. H., Rivara, F. P., Reay, D. T., Ferris, J. A., & Kellerman, A. L. (1990). Firearm regulations and rates of suicide: A comparison of two metropolitan areas. *New England Journal of Medicine, 322,* 369-373.

Smith, G. (1989). The effects of tobacco advertising on children. *British Journal of Addiction, 84,* 1275-1277.

Smith, R. C. (1978). The magazines' smoking habit. *Columbia Journalism Review, 16,* 29-31.

Somers, A. R. (1976). Violence, television and the health of American youth. *New England Journal of Medicine, 294,* 811-817.

Sprafkin, J., & Silverman, L. T. (1982). Sex on prime-time. In M. Schwartz (Ed.), *TV and teens* (pp. 130-135). Reading, MA: Addison-Wesley.

Staffieri, J. R. (1967). A study of social stereotype of body image in children. *Journal of Personality and Social Psychology, 7,* 101-104.

Steenland, S. (1988). *Growing up in prime time: An analysis of adolescent girls on television.* Washington, DC: National Commission on Working Women of Wider Opportunities for Women.

(handwritten note in left margin: from p. 46)

Steuer, F. B., Applefield, J. M., & Smith, R. (1971). Televised aggression and interpersonal aggression of preschool children. *Journal of Experimental Child Psychology, 11,* 442-447.

Story, M., & Faulkner, P. (1990). The prime time diet: A content analysis of eating behavior and food messages in television program content and commercials. *American Journal of Public Health, 80,* 738-740.

Strasburger, V. C. (1985). When parents ask about. . . . The influence of TV on their kids. *Contemporary Pediatrics, 2,* 18-27.

Strasburger, V. C. (1988, July 31). Children need national TV network. *Hartford Courant.*

Strasburger, V. C. (1989a). Adolescent sexuality and the media. *Pediatric Clinics of North America, 36,* 747-774.

Strasburger, V. C. (1989b). Children, adolescents, and television 1989—II. The role of the pediatrician. *Pediatrics, 83,* 446-448.

Strasburger, V. C. (1989c). Why just say no just won't work. *Journal of Pediatrics, 114,* 676-681.

Strasburger, V. C. (1990). Television and adolescents: Sex, drugs, rock 'n' roll. *Adolescent Medicine: State of the Art Reviews, 1,* 161-194.

Strasburger, V. C. (1992). Children, adolescents, and television. *Pediatrics in Review, 13,* 144-151.

Strasburger, V. C. (1993a). Adolescents and the media: Five crucial issues. *Adolescent Medicine: State of the Art Reviews, 4,* 479-493.

Strasburger, V. C. (1993b). Adolescents, drugs and the media. *Adolescent Medicine: State of the Art Reviews, 4,* 391-415.

Strasburger, V. C. (1993c). *Getting your kids to say no in the '90s when you said yes in the '60s.* New York: Fireside/Simon & Schuster.

Strasburger, V. C., & Brown, R. T. (1991). *Adolescent Medicine: A Practical Guide.* Boston: Little, Brown.

Strasburger, V. C., & Comstock, G. (Eds.). (1993). Adolescents and the media. *Adolescent Medicine: State of the Art Reviews, 4,* 479-657.

Sun, S.-W., & Lull, J. (1986). The adolescent audience for music videos and why they watch. *Journal of Communication, 36,* 115-125.

Surgeon General's Scientific Advisory Committee on Television and Social Behavior. (1972). *Television and growing up: The impact of televised violence.* Washington, DC: U.S. Government Printing Office.

Svetkey, B. (1994, March 18). Here's the beef. *Entertainment Weekly,* pp. 26-28.

Tan, A. (1979). TV beauty ads and role expectations of adolescent female viewers. *Journalism Quarterly, 56,* 283-288.

Tanner, J. (1981). Pop music and peer groups: A study of Canadian high school students' responses to pop music. *Canadian Review of Sociology and Anthropology, 18,* 1-13.

Taras, H. L., Sallis, J. F., Patterson, T. L., Nader, P. R., & Nelson, J. A. (1989). Television's influence on children's diet and physical activity. *Developmental and Behavioral Pediatrics, 10,* 176-180.

Teen deaths from guns on the rise. (1993, March 24). *Albuquerque Journal,* p. A5.

Thomas, M. H., Horton, R. W., Lippencott, E. C., & Drabman, R. S. (1977). Desensitization to portrayals of real-life aggression as a function of exposure to television violence. *Journal of Personality and Social Psychology, 35,* 450-458.

Thornburg, H. (1981). Adolescent sources of information on sex. *Journal of School Health, 51,* 274-277.

from p. 87

Tobacco's toll. (1992). *Lancet, 339,* 1267.

Torabi, M. R., Bailey, W. J., & Majd-Jabbari, M. (1993). Cigarette smoking as a predictor of alcohol and other drug use by children and adolescents: Evidence of the "gateway drug effect." *Journal of School Health, 63,* 302-306.

Tucker, L. A. (1985). Television's role regarding alcohol use among teenagers. *Adolescence, 20,* 593-598.

U.S. Department of Health and Human Services. (1990). *Healthy people 2000: National health promotion and disease prevention objectives.* Washington: Author.

U.S. Department of Health, Education, and Welfare. (1964). *Smoking and health: Report of the advisory committee to the surgeon general.* Washington, DC: U.S. Public Health Service.

Vickers, A. (1992). Why cigarette advertising should be banned. *British Medical Journal, 304,* 1195-1196.

Vincent, R. C., Davis, D. K., & Bronszkowski, L. A. (1987). Sexism in MTV: The portrayal of women in rock videos. *Journalism Quarterly, 64,* 750-755.

Wakefield, D. (1987, November 7). Teen sex and TV: How the medium has grown up. *TV Guide,* pp. 4-6.

Wallack, L., Cassady, D., & Grube, J. (1990). *TV beer commercials and children: Exposure, attention, beliefs, and expectations about drinking as an adult.* Washington, DC: AAA Foundation for Traffic Safety.

Wallack, L., Dorfman, L., Jernigan, D., & Themba, M. (1993). *Media advocacy and public health.* Newbury Park, CA: Sage.

Wallack, L., Grube, J. W., Madden, P. A., & Breed, W. (1990). Portrayals of alcohol on prime-time television. *Journal of Studies on Alcohol, 51,* 428-437.

Wallack, L., & Montgomery, K. (1992). Advertising for all by the year 2000: Public health implications for less developed countries. *Journal of Public Health Policy, 13,* 204-223.

Walsh-Childers, K. (1991, May). *Adolescents' interpretations of the birth control behavior of a soap opera couple.* Paper presented at the annual meeting of the International Communication Association, Chicago.

Warner, K. E. (1985). Cigarette advertising and media coverage of smoking and health. *New England Journal of Medicine, 312,* 384-388.

Warner, K. E., Goldenhar, L. M., & McLaughlin, C. G. (1992). Cigarette advertising and magazine coverage of the hazards of smoking. *New England Journal of Medicine, 326,* 305-309.

Wass, H., Raup, J. L., Cerullo, K., Martel, L. G., Mingione, L. A., & Sperring, A. M. (1988). Adolescents' interest in and views of destructive themes in rock music. *Omega, 19,* 177-186.

Waters, H. F., & Beachy, L. (1993, March 1). Next year, 500 channels. *Newsweek,* pp. 75-76.

Wattleton, F. (1987). American teens: Sexually active, sexually illiterate. *Journal of School Health, 57,* 379-380.

Weaver, J. B., III. (1994). Pornography and sexual callousness: The perceptual and behavioral consequences of exposure to pornography. In D. Zillmann, J. Bryant, & A. C. Huston (Eds.), *Media, children, and the family: Social, scientific, psychodynamic, and clinical perspectives* (pp. 215-228). Hillsdale, NJ: Lawrence Erlbaum.

Weaver, J. B., Masland, J. L., & Zillmann, D. (1984). Effect of erotica on young men's aesthetic perception of their female sexual partners. *Perceptual and Motor Skills, 58,* 929-930.

Weidinger, C. K., & Demi, A. S. (1991). Music listening preferences and preadmission dysfunctional psychosocial behaviors of adolescents hospitalized on an in-patient psychiatric unit. *Journal of Child and Adolescent Psychiatric Mental Health Nursing, 4,* 3-8.

Weis, W. L., & Burke, C. (1986). Media content and tobacco advertising: An unhealthy addiction. *Journal of Communication, 36,* 59-69.

Weise, E. (1993, September 15). Home video game released in 2 versions. *Albuquerque Journal* [Associated Press].

Whelan, E. M., Sheridan, M. J., Meister, K. A., & Mosher, B. A. (1981). Analysis of coverage of tobacco hazards in women's magazines. *Journal of Public Health Policy, 2,* 29-35.

Williams, T. B. (Ed.). (1986). *The impact of television: A natural experiment in three communities.* New York: Academic Press.

Willis, E. D., McCoy, B., & Berman, M. (1990). The effect of a weight management program on self-esteem and body image in obese youth [abstract]. *American Journal of Diseases of Children, 144,* 417.

Winn, M. (1987). *Unplugging the plug-in drug.* New York: Penguin.

Wintemute, G. J., Teret, S. P., Kraus, J. F., Wright, M. A., & Bradfield, G. (1987). When children shoot children: 88 unintended deaths in California. *Journal of the American Medical Association, 257,* 3107-3109.

Wiseman, C. V., Gray, J. J., Mosimann, J. E., & Ahrens, A. H. (1992). Cultural expectations of thinness in women: An update. *International Journal of Eating Disorders, 11,* 85-89.

Wong, N. D., Hei, T. K., Qaqundah, P. Y., Davidson, D. M., Bassin, S. L., & Gold, K. V. (1992). Television viewing and pediatric hypercholesterolemia. *Pediatrics, 90,* 75-79.

Wood, W., Wong, F., & Chachere, J. (1991). Effects of media violence on viewers' aggression in unconstrained social interaction. *Psychological Bulletin, 109,* 371-383.

Young, B. M. (1990). *Television advertising and children.* New York: Oxford University Press.

Zabin, L. S., Hirsch, M. B., Smith, E. A., & Hardy, J. B. (1984). Adolescent sexual attitudes and behavior: Are they consistent? *Family Planning Perspectives, 16,* 181-185.

Zelnik, M., & Kim, Y. J. (1982). Sex education and its association with teenage sexual activity, pregnancy, and contraceptive use. *Family Planning Perspectives, 14,* 117-126.

Zillmann, D. (1971). Excitation transfer in communication-mediated aggressive behavior. *Journal of Experimental and Social Psychology, 7,* 419-434.

Zillmann, D. (1994). Erotica and family values. In D. Zillmann, J. Bryant, & A. C. Huston (Eds.), *Media, children, and the family: Social, scientific, psychodynamic, and clinical perspectives* (pp. 199-213). Hillsdale, NJ: Lawrence Erlbaum.

Zillmann, D., & Bryant, J. (1982). Pornography, sexual callousness and the trivialization of rape. *Journal of Communication, 32,* 10-21.

Zillmann, D., & Bryant, J. (1988). Pornography's impact on sexual satisfaction. *Journal of Applied Social Psychology, 18,* 438-453.

Zillmann, D., & Mundorf, N. (1987). Image effects in the appreciation of video rock. *Communication Research, 14,* 316-334.

NAME INDEX

SUBJECT INDEX

ABOUT THE AUTHOR

Victor C. Strasburger, M.D., is a pediatrician and adolescent medicine specialist at the University of New Mexico School of Medicine, where he is Chief of the Division of Adolescent Medicine and Associate Professor of Pediatrics. He is a member of the American Academy of Pediatrics' Committee on Communications and has served as a consultant to the National PTA on children and the media. He is also the author of *Getting Your Kids to Say No in the '90s When You Said Yes in the '60s* (1993).